LIVING
RETRO

LIVING RETRO

andrew weaving *with photography by* andrew wood

RYLAND
PETERS
& SMALL

LONDON NEW YORK

Senior designer Paul Tilby

Commissioning editor Annabel Morgan

Location research Andrew Weaving,
                      Jess Walton

Production manager Patricia Harrington

Art director Leslie Harrington

Publishing director Alison Starling

First published in the United States in 2008
by Ryland Peters & Small
519 Broadway, 5th Floor
New York, NY 10012
www.rylandpeters.com

Text copyright © Andrew Weaving 2008
Design and photographs copyright
© Ryland Peters & Small 2008

10 9 8 7 6 5 4 3 2 1

ISBN: 978 1 84597 619 9

Library of Congress Cataloging-in-Publication Data

Weaving, Andrew.
  Living retro / Andrew Weaving ; with photography by
Andrew Wood.
      p. cm.
  Includes index.
  ISBN 978-1-84597-614-9
  1. Interior decoration--History--20th century. 2.
Interior decoration
accessories. I. Title.

  NK1980.W43 2008
  747--dc22

2007047381

Printed and bound in China.

contents

THIS PAGE **Mixing mid-century pieces with contemporary and classical detailing gives a home its own identity and is very living retro.** Here, a Herman Miller-production Eames lounger and ottoman are upholstered in white leather, bringing the iconic pieces bang up to date. The plastic wall panels echo the original door moldings.

OPPOSITE A Serge Mouille 'Conque' wall sconce dating from 1954 lights up the entrance hall of a Paris home.

It's a conundrum: now we are well and truly into the twenty-first century, why do we still look back to find inspiration for a truly modern way of living? It's ironic that we look to the past to create interiors that are in the vanguard of fashion. But, without a doubt, retro style still has enormous appeal.

Today our homes are an extension of who we are; a way of signaling to others our tastes, opinions, and outlook on the world. Of course, there are those who slavishly follow trends, with a new wardrobe every season, and an updated color scheme and home accessories to match, but equally there are also many who want to develop their own style and refuse to be dictated to by glossy magazines or retail superstores.

Living retro does not demand close adherence to any particular set of style rules. There are no limits other than the chronological parameters the look spans, roughly from the 1950s to the late 1970s. Instead, living retro is a multifaceted look that ranges from sophisticated glamour to pared-down chic, allowing its followers to cherry-pick their favorite pieces from the cream of twentieth-century design. It's not a trend that can be summed up in a sentence or two, but an idiosyncratic style that's all about having the confidence to live with the things we love, and to put them together in a way that suits our own particular circumstances. And at its heart is an abiding passion for vintage furniture and an understanding of the very best of twentieth-century design.

Those who choose to live retro generally fall into one of three main categories. First there are the purists—perfectionists who seek to recreate a specific moment in time in their home, and to put together an interior that is entirely faithful to the building that houses it, so the whole interior conjures up one look, one era, one moment in architectural and design history. Alternatively, you may have a certain signature style of your own, and this trademark look will be stamped upon your home, no matter how often you move, or

ABOVE **This furniture grouping in David Jimenez's house in Palm Springs is a perfect illustration of Jimenez's signature style, which draws on the popular Hollywood Regency look: an eclectic mix of elements from different continents and periods inspired by designer luminaries such as David Hicks and Billy Baldwin.**

OPPOSITE **A bold, dramatic black and gold wallpaper—Imperial Trellis by Stark Wallcoverings—brings glamour to the guest bedroom in David Jimenez's house. The unusual metal lamp, with its sculptural forms, ties in with the color scheme while adding another layer of pattern and texture.**

where you may go. Finally, there are the maximalists among us, magpies who have a passion for collecting vintage pieces and playfully and proudly displaying our favorite finds. Do you recognize yourself? Whichever category you fall into, you are living retro.

The purists' take on retro living may seem extreme to some, but the natural approach to others. If you're working with a mid-century home that has many original features intact, one way to go is to choose only those furnishings and finishes that would have been used at the time of construction. This rigorous approach to living retro can be time-consuming, as you turn into a design detective and find yourself hunting high and low for the perfect vintage fabric or reconditioned refrigerator, but ultimately these efforts are worthwhile, since it's the amazing attention to detail that make these homes work.

Purists dream of stumbling across a one-off mid-century house designed for an enlightened client, like my house in Lakeland, Florida (pages 120–127). Their ideal home is an untouched gem with its original features largely intact, having been loved and cherished by its owners, passed down in the family and well maintained—just like Courtney and Joy Newman's house in Palm Springs (pages 12–19), which had its original bathrooms still in place. Living in a purist retro home can be compared to living in a museum—some of us dream about it, while others shudder at the very thought!

If you love all things retro, but don't enjoy playing by the rules, the likelihood is that you have developed your own signature style and that your home reflects your personal taste. Homes like those of Jonathan Adler (pages 48–55) or David Jimenez (pages 80–87) put a very personal spin on living retro. Although the building blocks of these interiors are retro pieces and a retro sensibility, their owners have married together a combination of different elements and styles from different decades, creating eclectic and quirky effects. The provenance or production history of a piece does not matter if its aesthetics appeal.

The great benefit of taking a less historically rigorous approach is that you can see your home as a blank canvas, and it can be taken to pieces and then extensively remodeled to meet your own individual wants and needs, even if this means the finished interior is not authentic by the purists' standards. For example, Mark Davis's home in Palm Springs (pages 38–47) was extensively remodeled to make the space more suitable for modern living and to fulfil Davis's vision of the perfect retro home, one where original pieces sit happily alongside contemporary items that share the same feel.

The collector's home is another way of living retro, and of creating a home that reveals its owner's predilection for one particular aspect of retro design. This passion may be for a particular kind of artwork, like the Brian Willsher sculptures I display in my London home (pages 30–37) or Dubi Silverstein's collection of vintage travel posters (pages 138–145). Other collectors may have built up a collection of vintage furniture that they are obsessive about, a case in point being Nicolas Hug and his treasured original Scandinavian pieces (pages 21–29). Collectors' homes afford a fascinating glimpse into their inhabitants' interests and enthusiasms.

One of the greatest advantages about retro living nowadays is the wealth of pieces that are available. There are of course original pieces, many of which are now hugely sought after, from auctions, vintage furniture stores, or which may even be a lucky thrift-store find (increasingly rare, nowadays). There are licensed modern re-editions, as well as newer versions of twentieth-century designs or modern pieces inspired by retro or mid-century modern style. I hope the list of resources at the end of this book (pages 154–155) will provide you with a starting point for your own adventures in living retro. Nowadays we are lucky—the easy availability of so many fabulous retro and retro-inspired items allows us to create our very own take on retro style, using the very best of what's on offer.

OPPOSITE **An entrance hall or lobby is an ideal space to display a cherished collection of vintage paintings. Hanging them as a group creates more impact. This area was originally closed off from the rest of the interior. The dividing wall was partly removed and LS sculptural ceramic elements from Architectural Pottery designed by Malcolm Leland in the 1950s were installed, creating a screen but retaining an open-plan feel.**

ABOVE **An otherwise all-white space is the perfect backdrop for a collection of objects united by their vibrant tomato-red hue: Zsolnay ceramics, Holmegaard glass, and a sculptural 1950's Italian chair. The chunky custom-built shelves are ideal for showcasing collections of smaller pieces.**

THIS PAGE **The Newmans' favorite pieces in the house—an Eero Saarinen Tulip table and chairs by Knoll—enjoy pride of place on the raised dining area.**

When a reassessment of twentieth-century design first began some years ago, collectors were generally drawn toward the mid-century and, in some cases, earlier. The latter decades of the century seemed too close for comfort—less glamorous, less exotic, too familiar. Now the time frame has widened, and many of us are finding late twentieth-century design more in tune with our tastes.

In Rancho Mirage, just east of Palm Springs, Courtney and Joy Newman live in a 1969 house that is filled with an ever-changing collection of retro furnishings of the same vintage. Full of color and texture, this house bears all the hallmarks of the late 1960s and early 1970s—shag-pile carpets; sophisticated leather, steel, and glass furniture; and exuberant use of bold color and pattern.

Courtney Newman's passion for twentieth-century design infuses both his private and professional lives. Newman's Palm Springs store, Modernway, specializes in high-end vintage furniture and accessories; in particular, works by Vladimir Kagan, Milo Baughman, Thayer Coggin, Sergio Rodrigues, and Pierre Cardin, as well as items by Arthur Elrod, the interior decorator who worked on many of the large houses built in Palm Springs and the surrounding area in the 1960s and 1970s, particularly homes designed by architect William Cody.

The Newmans' home in Rancho Mirage was designed by William Cody in 1969, and is located on the grounds of the Tamarisk Country Club, which was established in 1952 (the club, on Frank Sinatra Drive, is the second oldest in the desert). One of a small group of houses, it nestles on the very edge of the club's golf course. Occupying an almost square plan, the accommodation is on two levels and surrounds an open central courtyard, with the master bedroom and main living areas having access to both this courtyard and the garden, which is adjacent to the fairway.

BELOW **Color is a big element in this house. In the courtyard the walls are painted by Ryan Alonsio, and the 1969 Bouloum loungers are by Olivier Mourgue.**

BOTTOM RIGHT **More color in the den, where the psychedelic padded walls enclose it and make it soundproof.**

BOTTOM LEFT **A retro mirrored wall sculpture reflects vintage colored glass decanters displayed in the bar area.**

The house overlooks the manicured green of the Tamarisk Country Club. The glass walls are shaded by the ample roof overhang. On the tiled floor that runs throughout the living areas stands a set of furniture from Pace Collection dating from 1970. The menagerie of animal figures, including a proud lion by Italian ceramicist Guido Gambone, sits on a custom-designed table by interior decorator Arthur Elrod.

The feature fireplace is clad with Utah Ice rock, giving a fragility and translucency to the chimney breast. The tubular chrome and squashy leather furniture grouped around the fireplace is by Italian architect/designer Guido Faleschini. The table is covered with a collection of glass *objets* ranging from penguins to abstract owls. The vintage floor lamp snakes over the seating to spotlight the sparkling glass below.

THE LIVING ROOM IS FURNISHED WITH EARLY 1970'S FURNITURE AND ACCESSORIES SET IN SOCIABLE AND INVITING GROUPINGS.

The Newmans are only the second owners of the house and were
lucky to find it with almost all its original details intact. The most they
had to do was to source and install vintage appliances in the kitchen to
replace the modern ones that the previous owners had put in, which were
not visually compatible or in keeping with the rest of the space.

Apart from this, all the original fixtures remain unchanged. The
bathrooms—one orange and one a vibrant, sunshiny yellow—are period
pieces. The yellow bathroom leads off the master bedroom, which is hung
with the original design of wallpaper that was chosen when the house

was built. The Newmans had the wallpaper reprinted
especially for this room, to match the original fabric
of the vintage bedcover.

The living room is on a lower level than the rest of
the house, a design detail that is typical of homes of
this era. With floor-to-ceiling windows overlooking the
manicured green lawns of the golf course, it is
furnished with early 1970's furniture set in sociable
groupings. Thoughtfully arranged collections of

FAR LEFT Pattern is everything in the master bedroom. The wallpaper, originally designed by architect Richard Himmel in 1969, was especially reprinted for this room to recreate its unique decoration. The bedcover is the original.

LEFT The egg-yolk yellow bathroom is also original to the house. His and hers vanities are divided by a mirrored wall. The room is flooded with light from the skylights above.

BELOW LEFT In the bedroom, an acid yellow armchair and ottoman are truly vintage, while the giant plasma screen brings this room up to date.

BELOW More bold color in the dressing room. This house is unique, in that it has all its original fixtures in place—a rare find nowadays.

ornamental pieces add personality to the interior. The Newmans' favorite pieces are the Eero Saarinen Tulip table and chair group—the first items of mid-century furniture that they purchased, twenty years ago—which take pride of place on the raised dining area. These items are of great sentimental value and will not be parted with, even though many pieces are only passing through on their way to or from the store.

Courtney Newman is fortunate, indeed—being a dealer in the finest of twentieth-century design enables him to constantly introduce new pieces, making this home a showcase of late 1960's to early 1970's design.

OPPOSITE **The view from the daytime lounge area toward the office space. The chair is the Hans Wegner Flag Halyard design, dating from the 1950s. The use of chromed steel for its framework is atypical of Wegner's work.**

TOP **The Poul Kjaerholm PK51 table doubles as a desk when necessary. The PK11 chairs are also by Kjaerholm and, like the table, date from 1957.**

ABOVE **Curvacious Swedish ceramics by Stig Lindberg, Gunnar Nylund, and Carl-Harry Stalhane fill the shelves.**

Living in Paris, you might expect a collector of twentieth-century design with a passion for living retro to focus on French modernist designers, like Jean Prouvé, Charlotte Perriand, or Le Corbusier. But the owner of this spacious converted loft apartment defies all those expectations.

In 2000, Nicolas Hug opened a collector's paradise in the St. Germain area of Paris—La Galerie Scandinave. The gallery, which has now closed, specialized in Scandinavian design between 1950 and 1970. Hug's gallery carried pieces by Scandinavian design superstars such as Hans Wegner, Arne Jacobsen, Finn Juhl, Poul Henningsen, and Bruno Mathsson, as well as the work of many lesser-known Scandinavian designers.

As you might expect, Nicolas Hug's home in the St. Denis area of Paris is the perfect demonstration of the delights of living with the finest of twentieth-century Scandinavian design. His apartment is a converted crystal manufacturing workshop built in the 1880s. A wide, shallow space spread over three floors, it has at its core the building's original wood and iron staircase, which both connects and divides the space.

Hug designed an enclosed entrance lobby, which divides the ground floor into two separate areas, a living area and an office space. The living area, with a Pierre Guariche sofa and chairs upholstered in zingy lemon yellow, is situated beneath the original workshop skylight, while at the other end of the space a table and chairs by Poul Kjaerholm is put into

The glass-roofed area of the one-time crystal factory is now a leafy lounging area at street level. The citrus-bright seating is by Pierre Guariche and dates from the 1950s, while the ceramic-topped nesting tables are by Roger Capron: part of the Navette series produced in the 1970s at Vallauris, France. The tabletop sculpture is after Alexander Calder.

NICOLAS HUG'S HOME IN THE ST. DENIS AREA OF PARIS IS THE PERFECT DEMONSTRATION OF THE DELIGHTS OF LIVING WITH THE FINEST TWENTIETH-CENTURY SCANDINAVIAN DESIGN.

service as a desk when needed. Lighting in the entrance area is by Serge Mouille.

In order to bring much-needed light to the lower floor, Hug created an atrium, an open space that runs almost the full length of the front of the building and allows light to flood into the basement. The bedrooms are upstairs, while downstairs is the kitchen and a seductive "chill-out" lounge with a nightclub vibe.

ABOVE The entrance lobby is hidden behind the display shelves and storage space on the right. The low black leather Pierre Paulin easy chairs are by Artifort, designed in 1959.

FAR LEFT The crystal factory's original wooden staircase rises up to the next level. Underneath stands a sculpture by Sébàstien Kito and a chair by Roger Tallon from 1965.

LEFT Curvaceous, organic Serge Mouille wall sconces flank the doorway from the small self-contained entrance lobby.

OPPOSITE In the kitchen/dining area, the Superellipse table, designed by Piet Hein and Bruno Mathsson in 1968, is surrounded by rosewood-veneered Series 7 chairs by Arne Jacobsen.

Downstairs, adjacent to the dining area, the chill-out lounge, with its ever-changing concealed lighting, boasts colorful lounging furniture by Pierre Paulin. The low, undulating sofas were designed in 1969, and the 577 easy chair in 1967. The squashy cream leather Elda armchairs are by Joe Colombo and date from 1963. Suspended in the center is Verner Panton's VP Globe, and on the wall hangs work by Jean-Baptiste Huynh.

THIS PAGE **The Arne Jacobsen 4130 chair drawn up to the desk was awarded the top prize at the Milan Triennale in 1957. Since then, it has gone by the name of the Grand Prix chair. This example has wooden legs, but metal-legged versions are also available.**

The kitchen is home to a Piet Hein and Bruno Mathsson dining table and Arne Jacobsen chairs and lighting. The lounge boasts squashy cream leather chairs by Colombo, seating by Pierre Paulin, and a Verner Panton light. It has recessed color-change lighting to alter the mood, and a music system so Hug can spin his discs. This basement room is cavernous in feel, thanks to the steel beams on show. The white and wood-paneled walls appear to float, due to the concealed lighting installed behind them.

Hug says, "I like eclecticism and wanted to have a quiet design space with straight lines for the daytime living room, with yellow accents, and a dreamy night-time room for the evening, full of poetry, with curves and organic lines in blues and purples."

RIGHT **In Hug's dressing room, a Pierre Paulin Ribbon chair from 1966 still flaunts its original psychedelic upholstery. The teak floor lamp was produced by Rispal, France in 1950, while the folding PK91 stool is by Poul Kjaerholm.**

BELOW **Hans Wegner designed the Valet chair in 1953. It initially had four legs, but Wegner changed the design to make it look less heavy. The sideboard, similar to the work of Perriand and Prouvé, is from the Cité Universitaire d'Antony, France.**

The bedrooms and bathrooms can be found up on the top floor. Here, a guest bedroom houses Danish furniture and a fine collection of tribal art, as well as metal sculptures by Sébàstien Kito. In the master bedroom and dressing room areas, more important pieces of twentieth-century furniture brings visual excitement.

Nicolas Hug's home is a quirky hidden gem, a labor of love. The eclectic yet carefully planned interior is like a tiny gallery with a collection of classic Scandinavian mid-century design on show. Hug and his partner, Philippe Menager, now work in real estate, specializing in top-end properties and, of course, incorporating design and furniture from Scandinavia into their presentations. Hug is also working with Pierre Paulin to develop a limited edition line of new furniture.

OPPOSITE British mid-century design and modern pieces work well together in this airy loft space. The Robin Day sectional seating, from the Plus Group, 1965, sits alongside another design by Day—the Festival Hall chair. The spider table is probably by G Plan. The cushions are by Jonathan Adler.

RIGHT The bent ply Robin Day chair sits on a rug embroidered by the New York-based textile designer Judy Ross.

BELOW A sculpture by Brian Willsher.

The notion of loft living first became popular in New York in the 1960s, where lofts originally provided cheap, spacious living/work spaces for artists. Nowadays, loft living is an option in every city in the world, and the use of former industrial buildings for residential use has become an easy alternative to the traditional home. Living retro—that is, living with mid-century modern design—is an obvious way to make a loft space a unique home.

My London home is situated in an old factory that once made dog biscuits; the studio spaces were carved out of the original space in the 1980s. The building has the distinction of being the first conversion of a formerly industrial building into residential properties in Britain. As a result, the spaces are generous, and the communal parts are particularly spacious.

George Nelson's CSS storage system, designed for Herman Miller in 1959, covers one wall of the main living area of the apartment. Perfect for storage and display, the unit is home to a collection of works by London-based sculptor Brian Willsher. Each piece is made from a single piece of wood cut on a band saw with some parts removed and some parts extended. On the table stands a ceramic vase by Constance Spry for Fulham Pottery.

THIS PAGE **In the den, a desk/sofa by John Pawson is all that's required. The Robin Day Festival Hall chair acts as a desk chair. The sculpture is "Totem"— a 1960s piece by Dennis Cummings.**

OPPOSITE BELOW **The entrance hall has an open-tread staircase, and a glass-floored mezzanine allows light to flow through from the roof terrace above. The Hilleplan chest of drawers by Robin Day displays more works by Brian Willsher.**

OPPOSITE RIGHT **Above the desk/sofa, the ceiling rises to its full height. In front of the sofa stand four Robin Day stools. The desk lamp is by Clay Michie for Knoll.**

The apartment is arranged on three levels and provides the perfect backdrop for a cross-section of fine British mid-century design. Original features are not too abundant, but there are exposed beams, painted brick walls, large windows, and concrete floors. A thick brick wall runs the length of the space and divides it, which made decisions regarding the layout of the loft much easier. The principle of one-space living is hugely appealing, but everyone needs somewhere to retreat and nest in their home, and in this case the wall has dictated the configuration of the living area in a way that has worked really well. An entrance hall, office, and den area are ranged along one side, while the kitchen, dining, and living areas are situated on the other.

The floor of the hallway and kitchen and dining areas was slightly raised, to allow pipework to be laid on the existing concrete floor. The new raised floor is made from sheets of pale birch-faced plywood, which contributes to the clean, pared-down feel of the place, and works well with the retro furniture and furnishings. The remaining concrete floor has been

THROUGHOUT THE SPACE, THERE IS AN ECLECTIC MIX OF TWENTIETH-CENTURY DESIGN UNITED ONLY BY ITS RETRO FLAVOR.

painted a raw natural-concrete color—it was originally painted bright red and repainting it seemed an easier option than trying to painstakingly remove the previous coats!

Upstairs, there is a room off the half-landing on the staircase, then two more rooms at the top of the stairs are built into the roof space. A glass-floored area gives access to a small outdoor space. All of the upstairs rooms were more like balconies overlooking the area below, so they were extended to make the rooms larger and create more privacy.

I have been buying, selling, and collecting twentieth-century design for several years now, and moving from a Victorian row house to this space

allowed me to fall in love all over again with items I had owned for years but had never been able to appreciate fully. The George Nelson CSS wall units, for instance, running along a long wall in the living room, with the high ceiling above, are such a great fit that they look as if they were designed expressly for this space.

Throughout the space, there is an eclectic mix of twentieth-century design that is only united by its retro flavor. On the lower floor, furniture from Robin Day, G Plan, John and Sylvia Reid, John Pawson, and George Nelson sits side by side with accessories by Constance Spry for Fulham Pottery and Raymond Loewy for Rosenthal. The wooden sculptures are mainly by Brian Willsher. Upstairs, most of the furniture is built in, but there are additional pieces by the classic English furniture makers Ercol, and by Charles Eames.

I'd like to think that this is how the space will remain, but who knows what utterly irresistible piece is going to turn up next? One thing is for sure—the John Pawson sofa/desk in the living area will have to stay, as it was installed before the floor was raised in the hallway, and so it has now become part of the loft.

After much thought and experimentation, I feel the loft space is now complete, with just the right balance of vintage and more recent items. Each and every accessory has been carefully chosen to add texture and detail to an otherwise simple interior scheme.

ABOVE LEFT **The dining area is at the far end of the loft and is lit from above by skylights. The sideboard and dining chairs are by husband and wife team John and Sylvia Reid for Stag Furniture in the 1950s. The dining table by Jasper Morrison dates from the 1990s. Fulham Pottery pots by DeWitt adorn the sideboard, while the mirror was a flea market find.**

ABOVE RIGHT **A pair of stools by Frank Guille for Kandya flank the kitchen island. At the far end, the hand-painted silk wall-hanging by Yumi Katayama was found on an internet auction site.**

OPPOSITE **Sleeping takes place on a raised platform that was once an opening to the level below. A 1955 Ercol lounge chair and stool are in the foreground.**

Decorative Art in Modern Interiors 1969/70

DECORATIVE ART and Modern Interiors 1975/6

THIS PAGE **In the family room of Mark and Kristine Davis's home in Palm Springs, a custom-made contemporary sofa in orange Ultrasuede sits alongside a vintage end table that's home to a table lamp and wooden cat sculpture. The bold design on the screen-printed pillow complements the pattern on the lamp base.**

BELOW **The master bedroom is screened from the country club grounds by a white-painted pierced-concrete block wall. The table and chair are Danish.**

RIGHT **In the family room, two Bertoia Diamond chairs dating from the early 1950s sit by the fireplace. On the wall the Frederick Weinberg's Fencers hang above a floating planter from Davis's shop.**

BELOW RIGHT **In the more formal living room, two low-slung Danish chairs from the 1950s sit beneath a metal sculpture.**

Restoring a mid-century home can be time-consuming and all-encompassing. Trying to track down furnishings that are of exactly the right period, authentic kitchen and bathroom fixtures, or architectural hardware that's of the same vintage as the interior can be a lengthy and frustrating process. And, as many lovers of retro living will testify, it's easy to become obsessed with the detailing, decoration, and finishes when renovating a mid-century classic.

After a lengthy restoration of his previous home—the Kenaston house in Rancho Mirage, Palm Springs—Mark Davis decided to put his hard-won knowledge to good use and to set up a business to help others going through the same process. Modern Home, Davis's store in Palm Springs, sells everything you need to update, restore, or revive a mid-twentieth century or mid-century-inspired contemporary home. Selling everything from Richard Neutra-designed numerals to mosaic wall and floor tiles, terrazzo and cork flooring, carpets, architectural hardware, lighting, wall coverings, wall relief panels, period-style textiles, and some architectural salvage pieces, Modern Home also offers a full design service.

In the main reception space, the fireplace has been knocked through into the family room, making it double-sided, while the chimney breast itself has been covered with a Modern Home diamond-pattern sculptured panel. Two mid-century chairs sit opposite a contemporary Delux sofa from Futurama Furniture—similar in design to the classic George Nelson hairpin-leg sofa from the 1950s. The dogleg coffee table sits on a contemporary vintage-style rug, which sits in turn on the newly installed cork floor that replaced the previous ceramic one, adding warmth to the interior.

THE VINTAGE PIECES HAVE BEEN CAREFULLY CHOSEN OVER TIME TO SUIT THE SPACE AND FIT IN WITH THE FUN, FUNKY AESTHETIC THE DAVISES HAVE CREATED.

ABOVE **The entrance lobby was previously enclosed, but now the space has been made more open-plan and the entry is visible from the living area. An Architectural Pottery screen was used to replace the dividing wall.**

Davis, along with his wife Kristine, moved from the bay area to Rancho Mirage in 2000, and they devoted three years to restoring the Kenaston house to its former glory. This single-story flat-roofed house is one of the few remaining homes by architect E. Stewart Williams, and due to Mark Davis's painstaking and sympathetic restoration, the house still retains its integrity of design and materials. The restored Kenaston house was then immortalized in the

RIGHT An asymmetric wall unit from West Elm houses a collection of decorative pieces. This type of unit is both useful and decorative in its own right. The shelves and cubbyholes frame and give importance to the items displayed, such as the 1950s-style ceramic pitcher with abstract motifs on a white background.

OPPOSITE In the dining area, a 1960's chandelier hangs over a dining table all set for a retro supper. A glimpse of the kitchen can be caught through the half-open door.

LEFT The breakfast area features a Saarinen-style table and chairs set. The orange walls inject vibrant color into the space. The chandelier is vintage. Outside, the pierced-concrete block wall affords some privacy.

BELOW Looking from the family room through the living area to the kitchen gives a good idea of the house's layout. The wall of windows on the left looks out over the country club grounds.

W Magazine spreads of Brad Pitt and Angelina Jolie "at home" and has also been the location for numerous photographic shoots and even a reality TV show.

Next, the Davises bought a 1960's house by an unknown architect in the grounds of Canyon Country Club, Palm Springs. From the records, they discovered that their new home had been completed in 1965, so they decided to create a home that might not be authentic in all the details but was a snapshot of how it could have looked when first built.

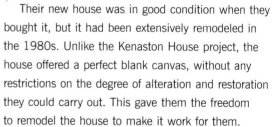

ABOVE **This house has plenty of vintage-style pattern in the shape of wallpapers and textured boards. In the daughter's room, the swirly wallpaper, Modern Home's 'Jukebox', pulls together the different elements: the desk lamp, the plastic Raymond Loewy-style cabinets by Broyhill, and the Pierre Paulin chair. The paintings are true vintage kitsch.**

ABOVE RIGHT **Different paper is used in the master bedroom, where overlaid rectangles are a bold motif.**

RIGHT **In the family room, a textured wall covering, again from Modern Home, is the backdrop to a white lacquer piano.**

Their new house was in good condition when they bought it, but it had been extensively remodeled in the 1980s. Unlike the Kenaston House project, the house offered a perfect blank canvas, without any restrictions on the degree of alteration and restoration they could carry out. This gave them the freedom to remodel the house to make it work for them.

"We took out the top half of the entry wall and added architectural pottery elements as a screen to create a division of space while keeping it open and stylish," explains Mark Davis. "The entire house was floored in white eighteen-inch tile, which we covered with cork for warmth. The fireplace was marble with a marble hearth. We built a linear brick wall and hearth, and opened the fireplace to the family room, adding sculptural panels to the chimney breast for additional texture. We added mica paper to the entry and one living room wall, and grasscloth to the hallway. We changed the doors to solid-bore birch and stained them dark walnut. We also added period-looking wall coverings to the master bedroom and the kids' rooms."

The furniture and furnishings throughout are a mix of original pieces and contemporary items that have been chosen because they have the right feel. The vintage pieces have been collected over time to suit the space and fit in with the fun, funky aesthetic they have created. The Davises have purposely steered away from the typical clichéd mid-century interior, so there are no Eames lounge chairs, Nelson lamps, rock-faced walls, or butterfly roofs. Instead, there is furniture in sharp citrus colors with bold, graphic shapes, set against a backdrop of authentic 1960's-style wall coverings and decorative accents.

Mark Davis's Modern Home aims to share his knowledge or and passion for retro interiors and furnishings, and with invaluable resources such as this one there is no excuse for compromise when it comes to restoring the mid-century modern home.

THIS PAGE **In front of the vertical blinds, a pair of Paulin chairs are placed on either side of a 1960's occasional table.**

OPPOSITE **In the dining room the walls have been paneled. The 1970's apple painting above the fireplace is from France. On the dining table and the low table to the left are items from Adler's Utopia and Muse lines.**

RIGHT **The dining table is from the Swag Leg line by George Nelson for Herman Miller. The chairs are vintage Richard Schultz for Knoll and date from 1961. They have been reupholstered in a re-edition Alexander Girard fabric. The globe lamps were custommade.**

BELOW **In the bedroom, the screen is a Barneys prop—a copy of a Warhol one made for a window display. The tray table is by Adler, as is the ceramic horse lamp.**

When I asked Jonathan Adler what his design philosophy was, his answer was "happy chic—it's about making design that is unimpeachably chic but not in a snobby or unpleasant way."

Adler is now well-known for his signature "happy chic" style—a studied, stylish elegance that is at the same time lighthearted, inviting, and witty. He wants people to look at his work and smile, and, walking into the home that Adler and his partner Simon Doonan share, it's hard to repress a huge grin. The whimsical charm, cheerful colors, and confident dynamic of the interior irresistibly draw you in and make you feel welcome. Adler and Doonan's many varied treasures are all proudly arranged and displayed with impeccable care and taste in such a way that the apartment comes together as a whole. The look seamlessly blends the familiar and the unexpected, and it's this harmonious mismatch that makes their home a very different retro-inspired experience.

The den, where Adler and Doonan watch television, includes many items by Adler. The Marcello sofa, Peter rug, Bargello pillows, and the ceramic greyhounds are all from current collections. The Louis chairs are upholstered in vintage fabric. The other items are originals, including the leather rhino, made by Omersa and bought from Liberty of London. The storage wall units, Storage Furniture Systems, are by Atlas Industries.

THIS PAGE The wooden slab table on the right was found in California and dates from the 1970s. On it sits a lamp by Adler. In the library area, divided off with Adler screens, Warren Platner 1705 lounge chairs for Knoll from 1964–66 sit atop an Adler rug.

OPPOSITE FAR RIGHT The office is home to an Albrizzi trestle desk and a Union Jack rug by Adler. The gloriously kitsch poodle lamp was found in Palm Beach, Florida.

OPPOSITE BELOW The simple white kitchen shows off more items by Adler, including a Utopia sun plaque on the shelf over the sink.

In a recent interview, after having completed the interior for the Parker Hotel in Palm Springs, Adler summed up his design influences thus: "I'm an eclecticist. I'm grounded in modernism, but not dogmatically so—I love the drama and adventure of Regency, I love the optimism of West Coast modernism, and I love to mix it all up... I would say that I have lots of influences from modernism, traditional art, architecture, and so on, and I put them all in my mental blender and they come out feeling fresh and familiar at the same time." Adler's own home is the perfect illustration of his inventive, adventurous design aesthetic.

Adler and Doonan, who is an author and journalist as well as the creative director of Barneys, have lived

"I'M AN ECLECTICIST. I'M GROUNDED IN MODERNISM, BUT NOT DOGMATICALLY SO—I LOVE THE DRAMA AND ADVENTURE OF REGENCY, I LOVE THE OPTIMISM OF WEST COAST MODERNISM."

in this location for about twelve years, along with their Norwich terrier, Liberace. They recently acquired and extended into the adjacent apartment, which has provided them with enough space to house their ping-pong table—table tennis being one of their favorite pastimes!

The original apartment showcased many of Adler's wares, but they were set against a very different backdrop. The great expanses of plain white wall were covered in a 1970's-inspired textured wall covering, a tobacco-brown grasscloth. The original apartment was once described as "Camp Baronial," and Adler's first purchase for it was a suit of armor... could it be the one that now stands on guard in the foyer at the Parker?

The "new" apartment is mainly white from top to toe—walls, floors, and drapes—providing a clean, bright backdrop for Adler's own pieces as well as an eclectic, almost quirky collection of retro furnishings. The only

ABOVE **Bathrooms are often blandly contemporary, even in retro homes. In Jonathan Adler's apartment, this is not the case. The tub is concealed behind a dramatic flowing orange shower curtain, while a large Hermès plaque brings a dash of glamour to the room.**

room with color is the master bedroom, which is all tones of warm taupe and a bold, mustardy orange. None of the original architecture was touched—indeed, in some areas more moldings were added, creating a faux paneling effect on the walls that compliments the bold graphics of the Adler-designed carpets, pillows, and bed linens that feature throughout.

The furnishings offer a cross-section of twentieth-century style, some pieces even earlier in origin, all updated with funky upholstery in bold colors. The quirky accessories reveal Adler's long-lasting passion for applied arts and crafts, each item being an important part of the home as a whole. Each object complements the next, with the bold shapes and strong colors insuring that no one piece dominates.

ABOVE **Upstairs, the master bedroom is totally Adler, from the bedlinen to the sunburst mirror. This is the only room in the apartment that has color on the walls. The ceramic horses watch silently over the vast expanse of the bed.**

Now with eight stores in the U.S., as well as an online store, Jonathan Adler has a huge following, and his crusade to bring glamour, color, and fun into our homes is seemingly unstoppable. His homewares line includes a complete range of quirky, graphic pieces, from furniture to rugs to lighting to linens. His selection of wares is ever-increasing, and Adler is now also working on interiors for other followers of his design aesthetic, as well as more stores and more hotels, all of them stamped with his own unique brand of "happy chic."

But above all, it's here, at home, where Adler and Doonan demonstrate that a flexible space, a happy heart and an unerring eye for fabulous design are the perfect ingredients for their own, very unique, take on retro living.

The structural supports of weathered wood add a sense of times past to the beach house and provide a contrast to the slick modern elements that appear throughout. On the right is the brick-built central core of the house, which encloses the bathroom, fireplace, and chimney stack. The furnishings include both designs by Alvar Aalto and pieces by Knud Holscher himself. A selection of his latest watercolors of the surrounding landscape can be seen on the wall just past the bathroom door.

Country houses have traditionally offered a temporary escape from the noise, dirt, and stress of city living. Whether you live in London, Sydney, Vancouver, or Helsinki, a country house offers a weekend retreat from the fast pace and humdrum routine of everyday life. In Scandinavia, the coastline and islands are dotted with summer homes that are as close to nature as they can be, many of them built close to the water's edge.

Danish designer Knud Holscher's vacation home is situated on the Danish mainland north of Copenhagen. Before building this house in 1995, the Holschers had spent fifteen years visiting the area, always staying in a traditional 1940's-built small wooden summer house. This worked well when the children were small, but once they became teenagers the adult Holschers needed their own space.

So, in a fir tree forest, they built this small, beautifully simple, single-space house. Heavily inspired by the work of the Finnish architect and designer Alvar Aalto, the space is reminiscent of the homes built by him earlier in the twentieth century.

ABOVE **The kitchen area consists of a wall of units and a granite island that incorporates two sinks. The curved ceiling, faced with birch ply, contains large skylights that allow plenty of light to flood into the center of the house.**

BELOW LEFT **The dining area contains an Aalto dining table dating from 1933 and still in production by Artek. Large expanses of glass provide panoramic views of the surrounding landscape. The sea can be glimpsed in the distance.**

BELOW RIGHT **A detail of the weathered wood support beams.**

The house is a single rectangular space divided by the bathroom core and the undulating wooden screen that conceals the sleeping area. Large glass windows run along both sides of the space; these have wooden louver blinds to lower when necessary. Aalto's iconic pieces are used throughout the space, their gentle curves reflecting the form of the ceiling above.

The Aalto furniture in the house includes his 1932 armchair 402, here upholstered in its signature woven black and white zebra fabric, the only decorative pattern that appears in the house. There are also two of Aalto's 1936 lounger 43 in natural webbing and his iconic tea trolley 901, which was first designed in 1935–36. The floor throughout is made from long planks of Douglas fir. On the right, the stove can just be seen, nestled into the curved concrete-block wall.

The Holschers recall visiting Aalto's Villa Mairea, where Aalto's son cooked them salmon and they used the pool and sauna. Villa Mairea was built between 1938 and 1939, and its curved, wood-paneled ceilings, use of natural materials, glass walls, and open-plan layout are all typical of Aalto's domestic interiors.

The Holschers' summer house, with its traditional weathered-wood cabin-style appearance, fits unobtrusively into the surrounding landscape. The location of the house is idyllic: perched high above the surrounding countryside, it enjoys sea views on three sides, providing a different backdrop every day and showcasing the drama of the ever-changing seascape.

The interior manages to combine simplicity, elegance, and comfort. It references the work of Aalto in its use of natural materials—there are distressed wood columns, plywood-faced ceilings, plank floors, and exposed brick walls.

The layout is extremely simple. The summer house is a long rectangle in shape. An undulating brick wall divides the entrance area from the living space, and also houses the bathroom and

THE INTERIOR MANAGES TO COMBINE SIMPLICITY, ELEGANCE, AND COMFORT IN TRUE SCANDINAVIAN STYLE.

the fireplace and chimney stack. At one end of the main space is the kitchen and dining area, while the other end is home to a small sleeping area, which is screened off by an Aalto flexible wooden screen when privacy is required.

When it came to furnishing their new summer house, the Holschers continued the Aalto theme, opting for his classic woven linen-webbing loungers, iconic tea trolley, and signature zebra-patterned upholstered cantilever chairs. Other retro pieces include re-edition Eames polypropylene Eiffel Tower chairs gathered around the circular Aalto dining table, and many pieces designed by Knud Holscher himself.

This timeless house is a tranquil and functional space—the perfect rural retreat for the busy city dweller to escape to.

THIS PAGE The lamp and bed are also Holscher's own designs. The end wall of the house is entirely occupied by storage cabinets. The freestanding screen was designed by Aalto in 1933–36 and is made from thin slats of birch strung together.

OPPOSITE An Aalto table stands in the sleeping area. The accompanying chair was designed by Holscher for Søborg Furniture.

OPPOSITE INSET The ends of the house are stacked with logs, all ready for the colder months. The exterior is painted black.

OPPOSITE **The house has high ceilings and a flat roof, so the fireplace and windows are all full height. In the living area, the fireplace is set high off the ground with a floating shelf in front.**

BELOW **Outside the kitchen window is a shallow shelf that acts as an outdoor bar.**

RIGHT **In the foyer, two tables by Marcel Breuer interlock.**

BELOW RIGHT **The flat roof and wide vertical slatted wooden panels (now replaced with metal slats), plus the thin clerestory windows, immediately mark the house out as an Alexander design. The materials include concrete blocks and sheet plywood. The lower roofline on the right houses the bedroom.**

Between 1955 and 1965, the mid-century modern housing developments created by the builder developers George and Robert Alexander vastly expanded and transformed the face of the desert town of Palm Springs. From the mid-1950s, the pioneering Alexander Construction Company produced a series of well-priced, inventively designed family houses in a new, sophisticated modernist style. In recent years, these "Alexanders" have enjoyed a reappreciation and are now highly sought.

Well-designed and solidly built, the Alexanders were erected on a concrete slab base using a simple post and beam construction. The buyer could choose from

The main living room area contains some classic pieces. The custommade twelve-foot curved sectional sofa probably dates from the 1980s, while the circular ottoman is likely to be a 1950's piece. The screen behind the sofa is vintage and was found in a thrift store in North Hollywood. It has been backed with fabric. The chrome-framed armchair on the left is by Milo Baughman, and behind stands a sculptural vintage Lucite lamp.

various different rooflines, including asymmetrical sloping roofs or a more dramatic butterfly design, which seemed to hover gracefully over the façade. The front elevation options included stucco facing, concrete blocks, or pierced-block walls. The Alexander houses also made good use of modern materials such as fiberglass or iron panels, rock-faced walls, or combinations of all of these features.

On the Twin Palms estate, just south of downtown Palm Springs, a collection of some thirty or forty Alexander homes still stand, many of them bought by modern design aficionados in recent years, and carefully restored to their former glory. Opposite the estate, nestled in the shadow of the mountains, sits the curvaceous form of Ocotillo Lodge, a hotel designed by Palmer + Krisel, the architectural firm responsible for the Alexander Twin Palms development. When it first opened in 1956, Ocotillo Lodge was the last word in modernist chic, and a popular destination for film stars and celebrities of the day.

This compact, tranquil home is located on Twin Palms Drive and is the second Alexander house to be restored by leading Los Angeles-based prop master Bruce Mink. Having worked in the film and television industry for

twenty-five years, Mink now devotes his talents to acquiring, renovating, and rebuilding modernist homes. He has bought and restored other mid-century modern homes in Los Angeles, and his main residence is a 1959 Steven Siskind house in Silver Lake, Los Angeles.

The Twin Palms project represented a huge commitment. When Mink bought the house, it was a dilapidated building, just a shell of its former self. Nothing remained of the original rendering that the architect William Krisel had specified for the exterior of the house. Instead, the entire façade of the house had to be painstakingly recreated, right down to painting the new stucco the original paint color.

It took nine months to restore the house. Everything had to be done from scratch. The original swimming pool was a hole in the ground, and was laboriously replastered and retiled. In addition to faithfully restoring the house from the ground up, Mink took the opportunity to make a few tiny tweaks to the original design. The rear elevation of the house was redesigned

The spacious master bedroom includes a selection of vintage cabinetry and upholstered furniture. The bedside table is one of a pair. On the right are the original built-in sliding-door closets, while on the back wall the high-level clerestory windows allow clear desert light to flood into the room.

to enlarge the vista of the desert sky, but all the other glazed areas remain faithful to the 1956 plan, as does the layout of the house.

Instead of approaching the interior decoration of the house room by room, it has been treated as a beautifully thought-out whole. The furnishings are mainly original retro pieces that date to around the

RIGHT **An inviting grouping of a Woodard metal chair and a vintage hairpin-leg table.**

FAR RIGHT **Another tempting seating group at the back of the house.**

BELOW **The kitchen has deep clerestory windows screened by the metal slatted panels suspended from the roof. The glossy vinyl vintage barstools were found in a Palm Springs consignment store. The triple ball light fixture hanging over the island unit adds interest.**

THE REAR ELEVATION OF THE HOUSE WAS REDESIGNED TO ENLARGE THE VISTA OF THE MOUNTAINS AND SKY, BUT THE OTHER GLAZED AREAS REMAIN FAITHFUL TO THE 1956 PLAN.

mid- to late 1950s—exactly the same time as the house was built. There are also some pieces that were custommade for the house, as well as some carefully chosen newer items.

The color scheme within the house takes its cue from the exterior landscape, utilizing muted earth colors for the paint colors, furniture, and upholstery. The subtle, soothing scheme employs a limited, luxurious palette that ranges from pearly whites to gentle ochers. The colors were carefully selected to provide, in Mink's own words, "a tranquillity as one resides in a desert home. I wanted very little distraction from the desert sky, light, and heat."

At the moment, Mink is pouring his considerable energies into creating a new, modernist-style home that will be built off-site, then erected on a lot in Palm Springs. The 2600-ft² home, with three bedrooms and bathrooms, will have sliding doors at both ends to blur the boundaries between indoors and out and allow uninterrupted mountain views—it will be, in effect, an Alexander home for the twenty-first century.

The master bedroom opens onto its own terrace, allowing privacy when necessary. The garden is full of white oleander. The deep roof overhang provides essential shade from the desert sun and is typical of the Alexander homes.

A desirable Arne Jacobsen tan leather Egg Chair for Fritz Hansen dating to 1958 occupies pole position in the upstairs living room, surrounded with carefully chosen vintage pieces. The languorous curves of the Aalto glass dish on the table balance those of the chair.

RIGHT A glazed wall separates the staircase landing from the main living room. The olive-green Eames lounger is of European production and an unusual color choice. The storage system behind is laden with retro pieces from around the globe, while the 1956 floor lamp is by John and Sylvia Reid for Rotaflex.

BELOW An A 335 hanging fixture by Alvar Aalto lights up the stairwell, while on the wall hang paintings reminiscent of designs by Verner Panton.

BELOW RIGHT In the spare room, a globe sits atop a vintage dentist's cabinet.

The aftermath of World War II witnessed a massive demand for new housing, both in the public and private sectors. All over Britain various housing developers and contractors were involved in postwar housing schemes. Most of this new housing was unashamedly modernist in its conception, design, and construction. Architects and planners were looking boldly to the future, using innovative new materials and creating functional yet elegant homes that were tailored to the requirements of modern living.

In Dulwich, a tranquil suburb of southeast London, the building company Wates was responsible for several new housing developments on recently cleared ground. On a site that had originally held large Victorian houses in well-established mature gardens, they constructed a new, pleasantly secluded development consisting of modern low- and high-rise housing set within the existing landscaping: "modern houses within nature, very Scandinavian in inspiration."

A Pucci cushion sits on an English sofa in the Danish Modern style by Greaves & Thomas. It is surrounded by key twentieth-century pieces. On the right is the Coconut chair, designed in 1955 by George Nelson for Herman Miller. The globe lamp on the right is another design by John and Sylvia Reid for Rotaflex, and the abstract-shaped wicker table is probably Belgian. On the left, the giant table lamp is by ceramicist Bernard Rooke, and on the wall above is a textile by Verner Panton.

THIS PAGE AND OPPOSITE **The dining area on the ground floor also showcases furniture by John and Sylvia Reid. This S320 dining set was designed for Stag Furniture in 1959. The cabinet, designed by Robert Heritage and with decoration by Dorothy Heritage, is from 1954. The hanging trio of lights is most probably by the firm Architectural Lighting and dates from the mid-1950s. The graphic red and white curtain came from the home of furniture designer Max Clendenning and his partner Ralph Adrons, and was made from colored rayon suit linings in the early 1960s.**

THE COLLECTIONS RANGE FROM FURNITURE BY ALVAR AALTO, CHARLES EAMES, GEORGE NELSON, ROBIN DAY, AND ERNEST RACE TO TEXTILES BY LUCIENNE DAY AND VERNER PANTON AND SOUVENIRS FROM TRAVELS ACROSS THE GLOBE.

While the development was planned between 1956 and 1958, construction did not get underway until the early 1960s. At the time, this house was described as "a split-level four-bedroom design, on five levels at half-story height." Of the forty or so houses that Wates planned for this development, only fifteen were completed. The materials used were high specification for the time, including Crittal metal windows, hot-air heating, Vitrolite glass paneling, and mahogany flooring.

When the owners of this house moved in fairly recently, they were lucky enough to find the original features pretty much intact. The floors had been carpeted, which had protected the mahogany beneath, and the windows were original. The kitchen and bathrooms had been updated, and the front porch had

been extended, but the new owners plan to sympathetically restore or replace these areas in time.

The layout of the house is reminiscent of a Georgian town house, with the main living area situated on the second floor, which gives the room more importance, like a formal drawing room. It also means that the living room enjoys a vantage point over the ever-changing wooded areas that surround the estate. The living room is approached via a staircase that leads up toward a wall of glass, while the dining area is open and inviting on the ground floor at the bottom of the stairs. The owners are avid collectors, and the living area offers a perfect display space for the owners' fine twentieth-century furniture as well as an eclectic collection of treasured artworks.

ABOVE **The upstairs rooms all have their uses—more space for more stuff! The small office has a wall of open storage. Drawn up to the desk are two Ernest Race BA chairs from 1945. An original Anglepoise lamp lights up the space when needed.**

RIGHT **An Aalto high-back cantilever Chair 401 dating from 1933 sits next to his classic three-legged Stool 60.**

On the ground floor, the kitchen and dining room open out onto a small private garden that leads in turn directly onto the communal grounds, giving the impression that the plot is much bigger than it really is. On the top two levels of the house are the master bedroom and three smaller rooms, all crammed with the owners' treasured possessions.

The collections range from furniture by Alvar Aalto, Charles Eames, George Nelson, Robin Day, John & Sylvia Reid, and Ernest Race to textiles by Lucienne Day and Verner Panton, all of which sit happily alongside an array of smaller hand-picked items that are souvenirs of the owners' extensive travels across the globe.

In recent years, mid-century housing has enjoyed an increase in popularity. A re-evaluation of this type of housing, whether it be in a planned development (like this house), a country house, or an apartment in a tower, is long overdue. Thankfully, it is now being appreciated and cherished by a new generation of enlightened owners.

OPPOSITE **The light, bright guest room has a "Put-u-up" bed designed by Robin Day in 1957. The bold, graphic cushion cover is by Stig Lindberg, while the curtain fabric is Linden, a 1960 design by Lucienne Day for Heal's. On the left, the tallboy chest of drawers (just seen) was designed by E. Gomme for G Plan in the 1960s. The house still has all its original Crittal metal windows.**

OPPOSITE **In the foyer, a mirrored console table welcomes you. The lamps are by Tommy Parzinger for Stiffel, either side of a wall sculpture probably from the Curtis Jeré studio. The painted stools introduce the citron yellow color scheme. The silver foil bamboo wallpaper is from Clarence House.**

TOP **The elevation combines pierced-concrete blocks and a stone-sided wall. A black greyhound guards the entry.**

ABOVE **Pattern and texture from the Adler pillows is echoed in the grid of the white fretwork screen behind the sofa.**

RIGHT **The kitchen has been opened up to the main living area, creating a breakfast bar. The chrome steel vintage stools were found while antiquing in Palm Springs.**

In Palm Springs, between 1955 and 1965, the Alexander Construction Company was responsible for the construction of a large group of mid-century modern homes that in effect doubled the size of the city. Work began on the Twin Palms Estate in the mid-1950s. The Alexanders, a father and son team, worked in conjunction with their architect, William Krisel of LA firm Palmer + Krisel, to create a cost-effective housing development that featured pioneering architectural design.

With economy in mind, Krisel designed a series of houses that shared an identical floorplan, but for each house the plan was flipped, rotated or reorientated, and the exteriors were given individual elevations. The result was a good-value housing development that looked more like a community of custom-built luxury homes. William Krisel was involved in every aspect of the design process, from the planning, construction, and engineering of the houses through to the landscaping and color schemes, as well as the marketing and advertising of the homes.

This Alexander house on the Twin Palms Estate (so called because every home had two palm trees planted in front) was discovered by David Jimenez well before the houses became the desirable properties they are today. "I always loved the mid-century modern aesthetic of the Alexander homes in Palm Springs," he says. "I wanted a home in the neighbourhood of Twin Palms because it was the first Alexander development and all of the houses are about twenty percent larger than similar homes in other areas of the city."

When Jimenez bought the house in 2001, it had been a vacation rental for several years and was in need of serious upgrading. Inside the house, Jimenez has taken the Hollywood Regency look and put his

LEFT Jimenez mirrored the entire wall facing the fireplace, creating a spacious effect. The stone-sided chimney stack matches the front elevation.

The main living room has a sloping roofline and high-level glazing providing glimpses of the garden foliage and blurring the division between inside and out. In this calm, serene space, everything comes in pairs. The graphic patterns of the pillows and screen introduce Hollywood Regency elements to the room, while the covered jars bring an oriental influence to complete the look. The stone-sided fireplace wall on the left was an original feature, while the mirrored wall on the right is a more recent addition.

THE DIVIDING WALL BETWEEN THE KITCHEN AND LIVING ROOM HAS BEEN REMOVED TO CREATE A MORE SOCIABLE AND INCLUSIVE OPEN-PLAN ENVIRONMENT.

own unique spin on it. "I was inspired by the chic homes in books by Slim Aarons and by the revival of Hollywood Regency by hip designers like Kelly Wearstler and Jonathan Adler," Jimenez says, name-checking two modish American decorators who draw inspiration from the celebrated English designer David Hicks as well as the leading lights of American interior design history, such as Dorothy Draper, Billy Baldwin, and Billy Haines.

David Jimenez has transformed his Alexander home into a vibrant, glamorous living space. The dividing wall between the kitchen and living room has been removed to create a more sociable and inclusive open-plan environment. The entire kitchen is white with splashes of egg-yolk yellow in the shape of accessories. The tiled flooring running throughout the house has been epoxy-coated white, providing the perfect backdrop to the adventurous use of color and

THIS PICTURE The dining area is adjacent to the living space. The table base is chrome, and the chairs have been painted and reupholstered in white Naugahyde. Throughout the living, dining, and kitchen areas the tiled floor has been coated with white epoxy paint, creating a clean canvas for the furniture and accessories.

LEFT The two guest bedrooms are visible from the foyer. The bold black-trimmed valances add to the graphic glamour.

pattern throughout. "I limited the color palette to black, white, and citron with a hint of blue in the shape of a 1960's buttoned sofa in the living room. The bedroom areas are carpeted, and patterned wallpaper creates a coziness to them."

Outside, the original elevation of the house is intact, its gable roof and clerestory windows flooding the interior with clear desert light. The pierced-concrete block wall at the front of the house acts as both a dramatic visual statement and a privacy panel. These concrete-block walls are a recurrent decorative theme of other Alexander houses in Palm Springs.

The house displays all the hallmarks of the Hollywood Regency style—ornate furniture, splashy colors, and metallic finishes—and exudes a bold, opulent glamour. Jimenez's imaginative use of symmetrical arrangements, adventurous colors, and graphic black and white accessories give his home a timeless appearance. The key to its success is Jimenez's light, confident decorative touch and the way the entire interior has been conceived as a whole, from kitchen to bathroom, floor to ceiling, entrance to exit.

OPPOSITE TOP LEFT **A stunning Raindrop wall sculpture by Curtis Jeré hangs above the bed. This is one of the most desirable pieces from the Jeré studio and dates from the 1970s.**

OPPOSITE CENTER LEFT **A black-painted mirror found in San Francisco complements the wallpaper perfectly.**

OPPOSITE BOTTOM LEFT **A large white-painted credenza provides more storage in the master bedroom. The tall lamp is made from Lucite.**

THIS PAGE **Floating over the concrete staircase like a cloud of soap bubbles are a collection of lamps salvaged from a hairdresser's salon on the Champs-Elysées.**

ABOVE **These anodized aluminum table and chairs originally took center stage in a 1970's meeting room.**

RIGHT **The weighing machine on the raised platform of the office area is original to the space. Levy-Trumet found the curvy molded-plastic chair on the streets of Paris at 4 AM one morning.**

BELOW **An enclosed roof terrace is a huge added bonus for an apartment in an urban location. Here, plastic furniture is arranged in a sociable grouping.**

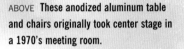

Looking for an old building to transform into an innovative modern home was a fairly easy option a decade or so ago. Whether you were looking for a barn or schoolhouse, a windmill or a factory, there were plenty of unused spaces just waiting to be transformed into an ideal living and work space. Now, the stock of old buildings ripe for redevelopment is drying up, and often any building occupying a decent-sized piece of land is eyed by big developers, who plan to raze it to the ground and replace it with something ten times the size.

However, some brave souls were in the vanguard of the vogue for imaginative conversions, snapping up historical buildings and fashioning homes from them, and Jean Pascal Levy-Trumet is one of them. In a north Paris neighborhood, Levy-Trumet, a stage and set designer who has produced

In the upstairs living area are two fine 1980's sofas designed by Antonio Citterio for Flexform. The structure of the building is on show here—concrete walls and concrete beams, the ceiling open to the rafters. Many of the items in Levy-Trumet's home are prototypes for projects he has worked on—the curved plastic balls, for example, were made for the 1998 World Cup. The mammoth fur rug covers almost the entire floor.

everything from fashion shows and installations to one-off promotions for new cars and perfumes, discovered a small light-industrial building that was once a metal yard and workshop producing medals, among other items.

Levy-Trumet took his time when it came to deciding how to structure the space. He devised the new layout and construction by paying frequent visits to the space and working out how he could get the best use from it. "I first emptied the space of all the different walls and panels to get to the structure, then I planted a tree in the garden and worked out where to put all the different rooms, staircase, entrances... regarding the light, sun, tranquillity, and convenience for work

LEFT AND ABOVE **In the master bedroom, the chunky shelving and the bed were both built in. The shelves are ideal for displaying found objects. The lighting was contrived from found objects, while the inviting leather armchair was "stolen from my aunt's room!"**

OPPOSITE ABOVE RIGHT **The corridor from the living room to the bedroom area is lit by a line of vintage chrome downlighters suspended on long cables.**

OPPOSITE BELOW **A concrete staircase protrudes from the metal-paneled wall, leading from the office up to the living room above.**

THE IMAGINATIVE USE OF CONTRASTING MATERIALS SUCH AS GRAINY WOOD, GLOSSY STEEL, AND UNFINISHED CONCRETE BRING A TACTILE WARMTH TO THE INTERIOR.

and for guests." When Levy-Trumet planted the all-important maple tree in the garden, the crane carrying it got stuck in the street, and this event broke the ice with his new neighbors, who even threw coins into the planting hole for good luck.

Levy-Trumet decided that the space would work best for him if each floor was used as a different living zone. The lower level houses a large open-plan work space, as well as the eating and cooking zone in the shape of a kitchen and main dining area. The work space and kitchen open out onto a tiny Zen-style garden that contains a small plunge pool.

From Levy-Trumet's work space, a dramatic open-tread cantilevered concrete staircase rises up to the spacious, serene main living area, while the building's original wooden staircase leads from the dining area to the bedroom and bathroom areas. The combination of the exposed original structure of the building with the raw concrete of the modern additions creates an understated backdrop to the diverse retro furnishings and artworks that are dotted throughout the space.

Moving from a smaller place meant that Levy-Trumet found that new, larger pieces of furniture were needed to fill his new home: "Having large rooms, it was difficult to find the

right-size pieces, so the dining table had to be specially made." Throughout, the high ceilings demanded lighting on a bold and dramatic scale. The lamps are from a variety of different sources— some of them were reclaimed from other buildings, while others have been cunningly concocted from found objects by Levy-Trumet himself.

Levy-Trumet's imaginative use of contrasting materials such as grainy wood, glossy steel, and unfinished concrete bring a tactile warmth to the interior and provide a varied backdrop to the minimal, carefully chosen furnishings. In the dining room, Mies van der Rohe's Brno chairs are grouped around a dining table by Levy-Trumet himself, while in the upstairs living space an aluminum, maple, and leather dining set sits alongside a sofa by Jasper Morrison.

Levy-Trumet's home is an imaginative take on retro living. The bold use of raw materials is softened by the forms of mid-century modern furniture working in harmony with numerous found objects that have been arranged as carefully as exhibits in a museum.

OPPOSITE **On the landing, a recent-production Le Corbusier chaise LC4 looks over a sylvan landscape. On the table is a sculpture in the style of Naum Gabo.**

RIGHT **From the outside, the Huf House is hard to date. It has a post-and-beam structure, large expanses of glass, and a wide roof overhang that creates shade.**

BELOW **Inside, the structure is all on show. Heavy laminated beams were bolted together to form the framework.**

BELOW RIGHT **In the garden, a mosaic by David Iredale creates an ideal place for alfresco eating.**

When your beloved family home of nearly four decades is in need of extensive repair, and you have spent four fruitless years unsuccessfully searching for the right plot on which to build something new, how do you finally reach the bold decision to tear down your beloved home? Easy! You find a truly sensational replacement—in this case, a Huf Haus.

David and Greta Iredale's previous home—The Woodhouse—was built by them in 1965 in leafy Surrey in southeastern England. The house was perched five feet off the ground, supported on steel stilts. The exterior was sided with diagonal planks, and the ceilings floated above the walls, supported on a steel frame. The house was completely contemporary, even futuristic, in its conception, construction, and visuals. And it was filled with treasured furniture and artworks that the Iredales had amassed over the years. Any replacement for their beloved home was going to have to be truly spectacular.

In the main living area, the painting and yew table with a geodesic base are both by David Iredale. The vintage sofa and armchair were given to them by a neighbor. The Eames lounge chairs and ottomans and the Arco lamp designed by Achille and Pier Castiglioni in the 1960s are all well suited to this contemporary house.

OPPOSITE The dining area is adjacent to the main living area. Here, the dining table and hanging lamp are both by David Iredale. The original Harry Bertoia 420 wire dining chairs and 421 Diamond chairs for Knoll both came from their previous house.

ABOVE On the end wall, Iredale painted a Mondrian-inspired mural that was inspired by the construction of the house, bringing strong primary color to the otherwise monochrome decor.

The Iredales were introduced to the Huf Haus concept by a design-conscious neighbor, who showed them the Huf Haus compendium. David and Greta Iredale were instantly intrigued. The Huf Haus met all their requirements—it was stylish, unusual, and practical, and their existing furnishings would work perfectly in the contemporary surroundings.

The Huf House is a novel concept: a custommade wood and glass post-and-beam house made in a factory to each individual owner's specifications. In the Iredale's own words, here is how the Huf experience works: "The house is preconstructed in Germany. There are thousands of permutations available, using different width modules, heights, and

BELOW The white laminated hi-fi unit on spindly chrome legs stretches almost the length of the wall. On the wall above hang plastic relief panels from Ikea. Above this area is the glassed-in landing that leads to the bedrooms.

OPPOSITE The retro-looking bar area divides the kitchen from the living area, yet keeps it open plan. Beneath it is a sculpture made by Iredale from offcuts of I-beams and floodlit from under the unit.

OPPOSITE INSET A view of the kitchen area from the entrance hall is typical of the whole house, with the strong verticals and horizontals creating endless squares within squares.

roof structures. Each house is completely customized. With the aid of their architects, you create the design that suits your unique requirements. When you sign contracts, you are given the actual key to your front door along with a glass of Huf Haus champagne. Then you go to Germany to determine all the finer points. The prefabricated sections are made, incorporating wiring, plumbing, alarm systems, electric blinds, and so on. The house is then transported to your site and put up in under five days. All glazed and the roof on, totally waterproof. Ground works and foundations have been prepared in advance. After erection, various specialized teams complete the electrical connections, underfloor heating, bathrooms and kitchens, and so on."

When it came to furnishing the house, the Iredales were fortunate. "Everything came from the previous house," they say. "We love it all—it was collected over fifty years." Original pieces by Charles Eames, Harry Bertoia, and Eero Saarinen sit happily alongside furniture and fixtures designed by David himself. Their collection of vintage furniture brings a unique dynamic to the house and adds a sense of

individuality to an interior that could have been blandly contemporary. All the artworks are by David Iredale, ranging from found-object sculptures to the mosaic wall in the garden. The "Mondrian" mural in the dining area is one of his most recent installations: it was specifically designed for the interior, mirroring as it does the architectural form of the house.

The Iredales are full of praise for their Huf House. They love the fact that the divisions between indoors and out are blurred, and that the house is always full of light, and they exclaim over the fact that after living in the house for four years absolutely nothing has gone wrong. They have found the Huf experience stimulating and fulfilling: "How many people live in their dream home? We'd do it all over again!"

ABOVE The main bedroom has deep sloping ceilings following the line of the roof. The end walls are fully glazed, giving the effect that you are amid the treetops. Accordion blinds drop down when needed. The simple bedroom furniture is upstaged by the reissued Mies van der Rohe Barcelona chair, which originally dates to 1929.

LEFT In the bathroom, a central tub fills the room, while the egg-yolk yellow Eero Saarinen Womb chair and ottoman (designed in 1945–48 for Knoll) bring a splash of sunshine into the space.

OPPOSITE **In the dining room, a vintage Saarinen Tulip table by Knoll came from Marcus's childhood home. Saarinen's fiberglass and vinyl 71 dining chairs were obtained via an online auction site. Above the table hangs a re-edition of the classic bubble lamp designed by George Nelson in 1947. The Ikea sideboard was "modernized" by the addition of hairpin legs, and above it hang architectural paintings of the RCA and United Nations buildings that were discovered at a Rose Bowl swap meet in Pasadena.**

RIGHT **The kitchen looks like it was lifted part and parcel from a vintage magazine. The floor is based on a design Marcus saw in a 1957 *Home & Garden* ad.**

BELOW RIGHT **Vintage accessories bring authenticity to the kitchen.**

Ranch houses are as American as apple pie—they are the classic American single-storey suburban home: long and low, with a low gable roof, deep-set eaves, large sliding windows, and an integrated garage. The exterior has little in the way of external decoration, except maybe shutters. Simple and economical, ranch houses were perfectly conceived and designed for postwar America, offering homes where happy families could live out the American dream. The style became dominant in the United States during the 1950s and 1960s.

Ranch houses have been criticized for their simple, often formulaic design. But, in recent years, there has been a radical re-evaluation of this style, and an acknowledgment that, at their best, ranch houses are conducive to convenient, comfortable, and informal living. Admirers rate the style highly, applauding its democratic roots and its practical approach to modern-day life.

The pale green open-plan living room includes a double-sided tiled fireplace that is a real focal point. The furniture includes Diliberto's favorite things in the house: a pair of Cherner chairs designed by Paul Goldman in 1956. There are also peices by Eames and Isamu Noguchi. The floor lamp in the foreground is probably by Lightolier. At the windows, vintage-style fabrics continue the retro theme.

ABOVE **The chimney breast is covered with translucent mosaic tiles. On it hangs a vintage starburst clock by Westclock. The spun anodized aluminum wall light is French. From this angle you can really appreciate the curvy undulations of the Cherner chairs, with their thin ribbon arms looping around the seat.**

ABOVE RIGHT **In the den, the 1950's metal frame furniture with its spick and span lines was produced by the California firm in the mid-1950s. At the desk sits an Eames fiberglass chair with a swivel base. On the wall hangs a zingy orange George Nelson-style ball clock.**

This Palm Springs ranch house stands in Bel Desierto; a subdivision built just after World War II on what was the golf course of the El Mirador Hotel. Bel Desierto was part of the "Movie Colony," where Hollywood stars built winter homes in the 1920s. Houses in this area were designed by noted architects such as Albert Frey, John Porter Clark, and Culver Nichols, and motifs from their work appear in many of the Bel Desierto homes.

Andy Marcus, entertainment lawyer for Fox Interactive Media, and Ron Diliberto, a psychotherapist, bought this house in 1999. It took them nearly three years to slowly restore and renovate the interior, doing much of the remodeling themselves. Originally the house had a central patio, but previous owners had enclosed it to create a fourth bedroom, resulting in a series of small dark rooms and giving the space a sense of restricted flow. Marcus removed walls and windows in the fourth bedroom, installed full-height sliding doors to afford better views of the San Jacinto Mountains, and opened up the kitchen and family room to create an open-plan interior and make a focal point of the mosaic-tiled double fireplace.

THIS PAGE Sliding pocket doors roll into the wall to close off the den area. In here, a vintage fabric-covered hairpin-leg bed sits atop a shag-pile rug. The kitsch plastic accessories—the tripod lamp and genie telephone—were both bought on Ebay. The plastic Prince AHA stools are by Philippe Starck for Kartell.

OPPOSITE The cool blue master bedroom features white lacquered furniture from the 1960s. A re-edition George Nelson pear-shaped bubble lamp hangs above the neat white wood nightstand.

ABOVE The bright blue 1950's chair is typical of the period. A fiberglass and metal planter sits alongside. The vintage-look textiles used to make the curtains include atomic-looking symbols.

ABOVE RIGHT On a lacquered chest of drawers, a collection of glass items in mossy green and azure brings out the contrasting colors in the curtain fabric.

INTERIOR MAGAZINES OF THE MID-1950S WERE THE SOURCES FOR THE COLOR SCHEME, WHICH FEATURES COOL, CLEAN CANDIED-ALMOND SHADES.

In addition to being a successful lawyer, Andy Marcus is also a talented interior designer. When decorating the house, he drew his inspiration from interiors magazines and furniture catalogues of the mid-1950s to make sure the redecoration of the house had an authentic, retro-living feel. These magazines were also the sources for the color scheme, which features cool, clean candied-almond shades, as well as the quirky decorative accents and furnishings. The furniture is a mix of vintage and re-edition pieces, all bought at online auctions or from local mid-century consignment stores, thrift stores, and vintage furniture dealers.

The kitchen, with its new countertops and appliances, has a strong retro feel, thanks to its black, blue, and white tiling and vintage accessories. Inspired by kitchens featured in 1950s magazines, it has a linoleum floor laid in an asymmetrical pattern seen in a 1957 advertisement. The house's clean-edged and playful 1950's styling follows through to the outside space, which boasts a kidney-shaped pool surrounded with Knoll butterfly chairs and lounge chairs originally from the Lake Elsinore health spa.

In this classic ranch, taking inspiration from original reference material has led to an authentic restoration, retaining all the retro elements of the house, yet bringing it right up to date.

THIS PAGE **In the den, a contemporary sofa is positioned beneath a steel and leather French wall mirror. The large bay window is hung with white-painted wooden Venetian blinds. The pillows add variations of color and texture to the room, while the shag-pile rug adds to the distinctly 1970's vibe.**

RIGHT **The unobtrusive lacquered storage units built around the fireplace neatly conceal all the audiovisual equipment. The Eames lounger and ottoman for Herman Miller upholstered in white leather are a recent acquisition.**

BELOW **In a light, bright bay window recess, a French desk and chair sit under a 1950's Counterbalance floor lamp by Pierre Guariche.**

BELOW RIGHT **A collection of Italian colored glass sits on a vintage black mosaic table.**

What realtors like to refer to as "lateral conversions" are becoming more popular, even commonplace, nowadays. For those who live in a building that has been divided up into smaller units, or an apartment building with a suitable configuration, a lateral (or sideways) conversion offers a great opportunity to increase the space. And space is a great luxury these days, as square footage becomes ever more expensive—and elusive—in our cities.

Along with her husband, Steven, and her two children, the boutique owner Jane Collins has lived in this London location for many years. Once a rambling embassy building, it had been divided up into apartments. Collins' home was the segment of the original house that housed the former ballroom and opened onto the large garden. The space was full of wonderful original features—dramatic moldings, windows, doors, and paneling—that provided her with a fabulous backdrop for all things modern.

Collins was passionate about her home, but it was evident that the family needed more space to house their growing children and an ever-increasing collection of retro furnishings.

In the family room adjacent to the kitchen, a cleverly conceived wall of storage provides a home for books and more surfaces for display. The jointed lamp is a retro classic designed by Eduard-Wilfried Buquet in 1928. The squashy leather contour sofas are by DeSede. A marble-topped Saarinen table is surrounded by a set of Jacobsen ply and metal chairs. On the shelf behind is a painting by the Collins' daughter, Juliet.

So, when the apartment adjacent to her original home became available, offering half the size again of her existing space, it seemed to be the answer to their prayers. Knocking through to the additional space gave Collins and her husband three more rooms, a kitchen extension, and two new bathrooms.

Again, the new space was full of beautifully preserved original details. An obsessive collector and dealer, Collins has a natural flair for putting things together to create rooms that are both easy to live in and visually exciting. With the prospect of yet more rooms, spaces, and walls to decorate, furnish, and adorn, she was in her element.

THE SPACE WAS FULL OF ORIGINAL FEATURES—DOORS, MOLDINGS, WINDOWS, AND PANELING—THAT PROVIDED A FABULOUS BACKDROP FOR ALL THINGS MODERN.

The entire space, including the original apartment, has been remodeled to give a new, "more modern" feel to the interior. On the ground floor, in what was the original apartment, the kitchen and family room opening onto the garden has been updated, but retain the same vintage furnishings as before. The entrance hall was significantly enlarged, bringing an open-plan layout and more spacious feel to this floor. The formal dining area has been made more accessible by replacing the walls with three-quarter-height dividers. The final addition to this lower level was the indoor swimming pool.

Through the main living area and the master bedroom suite, you reach the new upper level. This was once the main entrance hall for the original house, and the imposing arches create a dynamic, airy feel. A media room on this floor, painted a shade of brown that seems to change color throughout the day, is the hub of the new living space. Here, the furniture is a mix of classic twentieth-century pieces along with contemporary sectional seating that is distinctly 1970s in feel. A wall of built-in storage incorporates a fireplace and plasma screen television.

OPPOSITE **In the open-plan lobby, a pair of French steel chairs sit under a line of chrome ball pendants. Just to the left, the three-quarter-height wall partitions off the formal dining area.**

BELOW **In the "new" area of the apartment, the imposing hallway, with its lofty ceilings, has all the original moldings intact. The 1960's Danish rosewood console displays favorite objects, such as the box in the center made from plastic laminate marquetry.**

ABOVE **The walls of the upstairs hallway are adorned with bold, graphic images framed in clear plastic. The artworks cleverly complement the intricate detailing of the original moldings.**

ABOVE BOTTOM RIGHT **The kitchen contains toys for the boys: a purple baize pool table. The tall stools are attributed to Charlotte Perriand.**

This floor is also home to two bedrooms for Collins' children. The new accommodation gives more space to the entire family unit, allowing the children an increasing sense of independence within the safe confines of a family home. Collins' fine eye for detail has combined two disparate spaces into one harmonious whole. The fine architectural detailing of the original house provides a dynamic backdrop to the selection of art, furniture, and collectibles that unites the home. Collins' collection spans seventy years or so, with eclectic examples of excellent design from the 1930s to the present day coming together to create a luxurious living retro home that's perfectly suited to modern-day family life.

OPPOSITE, ABOVE RIGHT **The indoor swimming pool is positioned in the original apartment and accessed via a plate-glass door. The abstract red glass door handles are Italian. Jacobsen's Egg chair provides a curvy counterpoint to the straight lines of the pool.**

THIS PAGE **In one of the children's bedrooms, an American 1970's Lucite and plastic laminate wall unit holds a multitude of teenage "stuff," from a Mickey Mouse toy to a guitar amp. On the left is a Le Corbusier Petit Confort armchair covered in orange felt.**

OPPOSITE This house, which has remained largely untouched since it was built in 1956, displays a wealth of features that were new and exciting for the time. For example, in the living room a walnut panel slides on a track set into the slate hearth, concealing a television set that has been recessed into the grasscloth-covered walls. A Pierre Jeanneret 1951 Scissor chair for Knoll sits alongside a 1960 Time Life stool by Charles and Ray Eames for Herman Miller. On the shelf rests an original 1958 Sunflower clock by George Nelson for Howard Miller. A floor lamp from a design by Giacometti stands to one side.

RIGHT The dining area is divided off by stained-glass paneled screens that are original to the house. The dining table is by George Nelson and the chairs by Charles Eames, both for Herman Miller.

BELOW The full-height front door opens onto sculptures by Brian Willsher.

Mark Hampton is a member of what has recently become known as the Sarasota School of Architecture; a movement that was started by Ralph Twitchell and Paul Rudolph in Sarasota, Florida, in the early 1950s.

Hampton (the only Florida-born-and-bred member of the group) was their first employee, but he soon left and opened his own practice in nearby Tampa. He has since built several private houses and commercial buildings that adhere to the ideals espoused by the Sarasota School: clarity of construction, economy of means, simple clear geometry floating above the landscape, and honesty in the details.

Hampton originally created this house for an elderly couple who wanted a completely modern home designed for their retirement years.

It may look completely contemporary, but the living room in this 1957 central Florida home by Mark Hampton is a period piece. Every item dates from the late 1950s, and the Florence Knoll Sofa 67, Vladimir Kagan-style tables, George Nelson dining table, and Eames chairs are all originals. The stained-glass screens dividing the living and dining areas are also original to the house. The kitchen is tucked away behind the walnut paneling on the right.

LEFT Sliding doors in the dining area conceal a large storage bay filled with a collection of Russel Wright ceramics.

BELOW LEFT The kitchen occupies a central position and is accessible from both sides, making it the hub of the house.

THIS PICTURE The original walnut-faced cabinets look just as modern as when they were first installed. The rare eye-level refrigerator is original to the house, while the 1960's drafting stool is by Charles Eames.

THIS PICTURE **The guest bedroom contains several pieces that are original to the house alongside items from local thrift stores and estate sales. The Harry Bertoia wide Diamond chair for Knoll dates from 1956. As this room is at the front of the house, slatted wooden screens have been installed outside to create privacy. The desk and chair by Edward Wormley date to the mid-1950s.**

EVERY PIECE OF FURNITURE IN THE HOUSE DATES FROM AROUND THE TIME OF THE HOUSE'S CONSTRUCTION— THIS INTERIOR IS A PURIST'S DREAM.

The house remained within the family until very recently, its interior perfectly intact, unmodified, and original—a purist's dream!

During research for a book he was writing on the Sarasota School, the current owner stumbled across this house listed for sale. The price was high, so he didn't even entertain the idea of buying it. But a few months later he looked at it again and noticed that the price had been reduced. He went to visit the house—a fatal mistake, as he immediately fell head over heels for its many charms: the house had all its original features, was so complete, and so obviously in need of a good owner who would restore it to its past glory. But the owner only became involved and eventually succeeded in buying the house after he had heard that an offer had been made by a buyer who intended to demolish it.

When Hampton was invited to come back to the house just after its restoration was complete, he could not believe its condition. "It is just as I remember leaving it in 1957, everything is here! Nothing has been changed." When first built, the house featured every up-to-date detail: recessed lighting, sliding pocket doors, a concealed entertainment system, and a floating fireplace with slate cantilevered shelves. The details are so entirely contemporary that it's hard to believe the house is fifty years old.

BELOW **The guest room's private bathroom has a mosaic-tiled sunken shower area. The travertine and walnut unit is original, as is the floor-to-ceiling steel and walnut towel ladder.**

When the house was put up for sale, the furniture was sent to auction. Fortunately, some items did not find a buyer, and the current owner was able to purchase them. The most important piece was the stained-glass screens that divide the dining and living areas. The original owners had had the glass removed from the steel frames and inserted into wooden casings on wheels. Luckily, the screens didn't sell and were returned to their rightful home. A new framework was made, using Hampton's original drawings and photographs, and the screens were reinstated in the original spot.

A few other original pieces were also saved: the Bertoia Diamond chairs, the walnut planters, and several built-in pieces combine harmoniously with the new owner's collection of original 1950's pieces by George Nelson, Florence Knoll, Charles Eames, Pierre Jeanneret, Vladimir Kagan, and Edward Wormley. Every piece of furniture in the house dates from around the time of the house's construction, thus creating a completely authentic retro interior that is remarkably modern in both mood and atmosphere.

The house is one large space divided by a series of sliding panels, which can be pushed to one side to open up the space as a whole or pulled across to close off smaller areas. The full-height sliding doors vanish into pockets within the partition walls. Decorative details include white-painted stucco walls and ceilings, walnut-paneled partitions, and grasscloth-covered walls. There are two bathrooms: one is marble lined and the other features green mosaic tiles with travertine countertops. The kitchen, with its walnut cabinets and white laminate counters, has a rare eye-level fridge that dates back to when the house was built and is still in working condition. The seamless terrazzo floor of white marble chips set into beige concrete runs throughout the house.

At the front, the façade is screened with lattice panels that act both as a decorative device and a means of providing privacy. At the back of the house runs a wide covered area with a small plunge pool at one end. A swimming pool is being installed, as is new landscaping that will afford more privacy.

THIS PAGE In the master bedroom, an ingenious built-in headboard provides practical, unobtrusive storage. The doors open downward and are operated with leather pulls. The hanging lamp is original to the house, as is all the built-in lighting. The partition wall behind the bed houses sliding doors that close off the bedroom from the guest room next door when privacy is required.

OPPOSITE **String and steel PK25 chairs by Poul Kjaerholm sit alongside a painting by the Holschers' daughter.**

BELOW AND BOTTOM **In the living room, design classics, including Le Corbusier's favourite Thonet bentwood armchair—number 209—complement Holscher's contemporary designs.**

RIGHT **In the kitchen area, Holscher's versatile custommade folding storage units on wheels can be opened out to double as display space and insure that the cook has everything he or she needs right to hand.**

In Copenhagen, good design stalks you at every turn. Denmark has excelled in this field ever since the Danish Modern look, which was characterized by simple, functional shapes, organic lines, and blond wood, first came to international prominence in the 1950s.

Knud Holscher is a celebrated name in Danish design. Having worked for Arne Jacobsen from 1959 to 1960, Holscher was Jacobsen's associate architect on the construction of St. Catherine's College in Oxford, England. Since then, Holscher has won a long list of prizes and awards for his designs for both Danish and international companies. Some products have become modern classics, such as the clean-cut Modric line of architectural hardware that he produced in 1966. This timeless selection of handles, bathroom fixtures, and hardware is still in production today. During his long career, Holscher has designed everything from lighting,

The downstairs living room contains many of Holscher's own designs, but the hanging lamps are by Poul Henningsen, and the 258 daybed just to the left is by Mies van der Rohe for Knoll. Holscher designed the sofa. The locally produced handmade bricks provide a timeless backdrop for the modern lighting and furniture. The spotlights are also by Holscher and were designed for Erco.

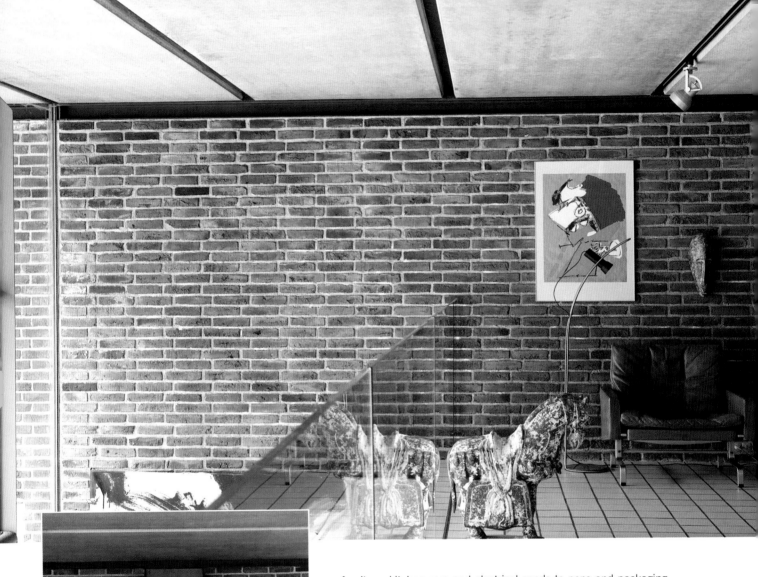

furniture, kitchenware and electrical goods to pens and packaging, producing timeless designs for manufacturers that include Husquarna, Georg Jensen, Erco, Philips, J. C. Decaux, and Pressalit.

For an architect, building his own house offers an opportunity to showcase his ideas and inspirations. Knud and Henny Holscher's house, in Holte just outside Copenhagen, was built in 1972. Now, thirty-five years later, the Holschers are still happily in residence, and the house feels as modern and fresh as it did on the day they first moved in—full of innovative ideas and visual stimulation.

The main structure of the house consists of two parallel brick walls spanned with concrete slabs that are reinforced with rolled steel beams. All the window and door framing is steel. The house is constructed mainly from a dark brown Danish brick, with the white mortar emphasizing the staggered bond design of the brickwork. It is set back from the street, yet on the rear side it is very open to the outside, with a double-height wall of glass that provides the main living space and master bedroom area with uninterrupted views over the peaceful, mature garden.

OPPOSITE ABOVE **The main bedroom area overlooks the living area below. The glass balustrade is almost invisible, allowing unobstructed views of the garden outside. The Kjaerholm leather chair PK31, from 1956, is original to the house.**

OPPOSITE BELOW **A small fireplace in the main room is flanked with LC1 Basculant chairs designed by Le Corbusier in 1928.**

THIS PAGE **The recently updated kitchen island juts out into the dining space. The glass wall opens out onto a small courtyard garden.**

The living room looks over the garden. The tiled floors bring uniformity and lightness to the space. As is always the case in Scandinavia, lighting is important, and the recesses between the concrete slab construction of the ceilings house track lighting.

A DOUBLE-HEIGHT WALL OF GLASS PROVIDES THE LIVING SPACE AND MASTER BEDROOM WITH UNINTERRUPTED VIEWS OVER THE PEACEFUL, MATURE GARDEN.

The house is entered from the side via a small glass box that serves as a porch. The glass front door opens directly into the kitchen area—the hub of a modern home. Here, the kitchen cabinets and appliances are housed in a single large rectangular bank of units. There are also four additional free-standing storage units on wheels, which were especially designed by Holscher for the house. One is a coat closet, two contain general storage space, and the last one houses the fridge. The pale tile flooring continues throughout the house, providing a graphic counterpoint to the dark brown walls.

The main living space is situated just off the kitchen and overlooks the garden. It's accessed down a tiled slope, with steel stair-treads attached at one side. This tranquil space offers a simple understated backdrop to several pieces by the giants of twentieth-century design: a Mies van der Rohe daybed, Basculant chairs by Le Corbusier, and Thonet bentwood chairs. There are also Danish modern classics, such as the PK chairs by Poul Kjaerholm and lighting by Poul Henningsen, as well as, of course, a selection of designs by Holscher himself. The large abstract artworks hung throughout the house have particular personal relevance—they are by Holscher's daughter.

The main sleeping area is situated just above the living room and also overlooks the peaceful gardens and the glassy, unbroken surfaces of two triangular pools. Here there are more personal treasures, including pieces of tribal art and oriental ceramics.

This house possesses elements of some of the great twentieth-century houses created by Le Corbusier and Philip Johnson, but they have been assembled in a way that has created, in Holscher's own words, a "great space with the advantage that corridors are nonexistent, adding to the feeling of a spacious house."

OPPOSITE The asymmetric shapes of the reflecting pools lead your eye out into the garden. The steel-framed wall of glass brings the outside in to the interior.

ABOVE LEFT The staircase from the kitchen to the lower living level is made from small steel plates applied to a tiled slope, while the one rising to the bedroom area has treads applied to a steel frame.

ABOVE RIGHT Woven chairs by Poul Kjaerholm line up along the central brick core of the house. The main entry door on the far wall is fully glazed.

BELOW The entrance foyer is a steel-framed glass box protruding from the main structure of the house.

THIS PAGE **In the living area is a boomerang-shaped 1950s Danish desk and matching chair. Original posters for United Airlines introduce visual interest and vibrant color.**

ABOVE LEFT **A quirky, typically 1950's French coat rack stands in the hall. The staircase rises to the next floor and acts as a gallery for Dubi Silverstein's travel poster collection.**

ABOVE RIGHT **In the living area, a vintage sideboard sits beneath 1950's wall light appliqués by Frederick Weinberg. A Saarinen Tulip table is surrounded by Eames fiberglass stacking chairs.**

FAR RIGHT **Just inside the front door, a 1950's Danish Modern two-seater upholstered in vibrant azure sits beaneath a poster for Le Touquet.**

The work of Charles and Ray Eames has inspired many, but to use their trademark ideas in the remodeling and reconstruction of a landmark preservation house in New York is a particularly bold and novel way to appreciate mid-century modern design.

Looking at the Eames house in California and the ESU range of furniture designed for Herman Miller in the 1950s, it's easy to see how various elements could be incorporated into a contemporary construction today. In Dubi Silverstein and Ellen Weiman's house in Manhattan, the steel-framed colored and pierced banister panels resemble the colorful graphic elevations of the Eames storage units, while the

The basement living room opens up onto a leafy garden, with shades shielding the room from the midday sun. While most of the furnishings are vintage, the main seating in the space is contemporary. The folding fabric screen references the concept behind the house: the Eames house in Santa Monica and the storage units designed by Charles and Ray Eames in 1950. On the left, floor-to-ceiling storage hides and stores everything.

picture windows in the lower level of the house recall those of the Eames house in Santa Monica, California.

Dubi Silverstein and Ellen Weiman commissioned architects Ogawa Depardon to undertake the reconstruction and design of the house. The two couples met and became friends in a children's playground, both couples having children of similar ages. Having already seen several of their projects, Silverstein and Weiman knew the architects shared their passion for mid-century design and their vision of the perfect family home. "Having spoken to many architects, with so many options and design possibilities, Kathy Ogawa and Gilles Depardon were the only ones in tune with us," says Ellen.

From the street, the house looks like a typical nineteenth-century New York town house, with a raised ground floor and classic proportions. But, once through the door, you take a step into the perfect mid-century home—one seemingly more at home in the Hollywood Hills than on a Manhattan side street. The interior has been boldly reworked to provide a clean, modern retro-inspired family home.

The entrance level is one large open space, with a glass elevation at the rear and a mezzanine that overlooks the lower-level reception room. The central staircase, with its Eames-inspired banisters, is the core of the house, and is flooded with light from a skylight above the stairwell. As you enter, on the raised ground floor there is a small parlor area, with a full-height stone-sided fireplace surrounded by a snug grouping of classic retro chairs: a typical element of a mid-century home, as well as a signature of Ogawa and Depardon's work.

The house is furnished with many original twentieth-century pieces, many of them produced by Heywood-Wakefield. This furniture has been greatly underrated in recent years, and it is good to see it play a starring role in such a house.

There were many different lines produced, including the very popular Modern line, and in general the blond finishes, such as champagne and wheat, are considered the most desirable. Using the pieces in everyday situations, such as the dining area and the master bedroom, brings an established and comfortable ambience to these spaces. In the dining room, the Heywood-Wakefield "Dog Biscuit" dining chairs have been reupholstered in mid-century-style fabric that chimes perfectly with the neutral tones of the birch.

The only contemporary furniture found in the house is in the basement living area—the prospect of precious vintage pieces being bounced on by the kids made the choice of a large, squashy modern sofa a logical one! This light, bright space is also home to a Danish desk and chair, and a group of Eames chairs surrounding a vintage Knoll table.

In addition to the original Heywood-Wakefield furnishings, the house is a showcase for Dubi Silverstein's vast collection of travel posters. Almost

OPPOSITE ABOVE LEFT The kitchen runs alongside the dining area and overlooks the living area below. Vintage accessories add to the mid-century look.

LEFT A set of original Heywood-Wakefield "Dog Biscuit" dining chairs and table from the 1940s are the centerpiece of the dining area. A vintage hanging lamp illuminates the table.

BELOW The snug area just inside the front door features a retro-looking stone-sided fireplace. A lounge chair and ottoman by George Mulhauser for Plycraft sit opposite a classic 1950's sofa. On the wall above the Heywood-Wakefield bureau hang Fencers by Frederick Weinberg from the same decade.

TAKE A STEP INTO THE PERFECT MID-CENTURY HOME— ONE SEEMINGLY MORE AT HOME IN THE HOLLYWOOD HILLS THAN ON A MANHATTAN SIDE STREET.

OPPOSITE **The staircase runs through the center of the house. The steel frame and pierced sheet metal echo designs by Charles Eames. A small table and chairs similar to Saarinen's Tulip line sit next to the banister.**

ABOVE **In the master bedroom there are more examples of Heywood-Wakefield furniture, this time from the 1950's Sculptura line. Roof blinds protect and cool the room from the sun.**

ABOVE RIGHT **The panels of the banister add color to the stairwell.**

RIGHT **In one of the bathrooms, a mosaic tile backsplash adds a vintage feel.**

every wall is adorned with these amazing pieces of history, which evoke the romanticism and glamour of travel in a bygone age. The collection has its roots in a trip to Europe, where Silverstein found that postcards of vintage posters of certain attractions captured his imagination better then traditional photographic picture postcards. Dubi is rightly proud of his obsession, saying, "My collection of airline posters was one of the three major collections used as a centerpiece of a book on airline posters, and at this point I believe that I have one of the most extensive collections of French railway posters ever assembled by a private collector." Most of the collection dates from the mid-twentieth century, but Dubi's favorite dates from 1909: "Palisades Amusement Park" advertises a park that he visited as a child in the 1960s, which was demolished in 1972 to make way for an apartment building.

In this remodeling of an older home, the pattern, color, and graphics of the furniture and posters have replaced the visual motifs—moldings, wallpapers, and *objets*—that have been removed from the house.

THIS PAGE **The dining area opens onto a courtyard area enclosed by a concrete block wall. Outside, chairs by Harry Bertoia surround a table by Richard Schultz, all produced by Knoll. Inside, Eames DCM chairs from 1946 surround a table that was custom-made for the house. Underneath is a rug made from interchangeable squares, creating an endlessly variable design.**

ABOVE While a concrete wall could be cold and uninviting, the color variations in these blocks adds warmth and subtlety.

BELOW The Brunsons' prized possession is this Eames red aniline-finish LCW chair. It sits below a molded plywood leg splint, also designed by Charles Eames.

When asked what inspired his fabulously retro Orlando home, Sean Brunson explains, "I spent summers in Sarasota in a Paul Rudolph home on Casey Key that was owned by close friends of the family. The Burkhardt house, with its raw materials, modern design, vast open spaces, and large expanses of glass, left a lasting impression on me."

Brunson grew up on the Gulf Coast of Florida and was exposed to the architecture of Paul Rudolph and the Sarasota School of Architecture from an early age. In addition to Paul Rudolph, the Sarasota School includes architects such as Ralph Twitchell, Tim Seibert, Mark Hampton, and Gene Leedy, to name but a few. Sean Brunson, the associate creative director of an Orlando advertising agency, and his wife Tricia are passionate admirers of Gene Leedy, who was Paul Rudolph's first employee in the early 1950s.

The Brunsons first approached Leedy about designing a house for them after seeing his own house and others in Winter Haven, where he had built a group of speculative homes in the mid-1950s for a local developer, Dick Craney, who wanted to build affordable contemporary homes. The Brunsons then employed a local architect to reinterpret Leedy's ideas for use today. Their aim was to create a distinctly twenty-first-century version of a mid-century original.

THIS PAGE Florence Knoll sofas create a sociable den area at one end of the living room. The wall units are custommade.

OPPOSITE An Eames lounge chair and ottoman encourage reflection beside the raised fireplace. The polished concrete floors have a glossy shine.

BELOW In the study, a collection of photos of family and friends creates a focal point. Below, two 1950's Eames chairs flank a 1957 Saarinen Tulip table.

The houses that Leedy designed in Winter Haven were single storey, of a simple wood post-and-beam construction, and built on a concrete slab. There were two different models: a smaller version with a central internal courtyard, and a slightly larger version with a courtyard at the front of the house. The houses were enveloped entirely in glass, apart from the end walls, which were built of concrete block and also functioned as a decorative feature within the house. One of these block walls enclosed the courtyard and linked the main house to the utility room and carport. Other important features were the strong verticals of the structural beams and the cedar tongue-and-groove ceilings. In addition, the front and back elevations sported full-height sliding aluminum-frame glass doors (they were among the first homes in Central Florida to include these).

The Brunsons wanted to build a house based upon Leedy's Winter Haven homes. The end result is similar in layout and spatial planning to the Leedy houses, but it is of slightly larger proportions, has a steel frame and more concrete-block walls. It took three teams of builders before they found the right ones to construct the block walls—the third team kept the block work clean and the joints well groomed. The full-height sliding doors are now of different proportions (due to hurricane requirements),

THIS PAGE The living room walls are finished with grasscloth, adding another texture to the space. Along the corridor are the bedrooms and bathrooms. The lighting is a combination of recessed downlighters and surface spots, creating different moods in different areas.

OPPOSITE-AND-INSET A solid wall separates the kitchen from the living area. With the addition of tall stools, a large island unit doubles as a breakfast bar. The cabinet doors are veneered.

THIS PICTURE Concrete-block walls are also a feature in the bedrooms. Vertical louver blinds hang the length of the windows. Above the bed is a painting from the Reynolds studio in California. This tranquil sleeping space combines both vintage and new furnishings: Eames Cats Cradle chairs sit either side of an Eames LTR table from 1954, but the bed is from Ikea.

OPPOSITE The Brunsons' daughter's bedroom opens onto its own small enclosed courtyard.

and the floors are made from highly polished poured concrete. In all, it took nine months to build the house, and it came in on budget.

The interior contains the owners' collection of mid-century modern furniture. They have been collecting for years, ever since those days "when one could actually find Eames pieces at junk shops and garage sales," says Sean. Most of the furniture is either vintage Knoll or Herman Miller, with the Brunsons' prized possession being a red aniline Eames LCW that dates from the first year of the chair's production. In the main living area, the sleek leather sofa and armchairs are by Florence Knoll.

The Brunsons and their daughter love the house. "The house has a great open-plan, even loft-type feel." The entire front and back of the house have huge picture windows that slide open, allowing the outside in and offering access to a patio area that's furnished with chairs by Harry Bertoia.

The Brunsons' new house captures all the soul of the original model, but can be enjoyed wholeheartedly, without suffering all the headaches of owning an older home.

RESESOURCES

FURNITURE, LIGHTING, AND ACCESSORIES

Jonathan Adler

47 Greene Street
New York, NY 10013
212-941-8950

www.jonathanadler.com

A collection of contemporary ceramics with a retro sensibility. Visit the website for details of their other stores.

Antik

104 Franklin Street
New York, NY 10013
212-343-0471

www.antik-nyc.net

Twentieth-century design and decorative arts, especially Scandinavian modern classics by designers such as Finn Juhl and Hans Wegner.

Artemide

46 Greene Street
New York, NY 10013
212-925-1588

www.artemide.us

The Italian manufacturer of many famed contemporary lighting classics, including Richard Sapper's Tizio.

B & B Italia

150 East 58th Street
New York, NY 10155
800-872-1697

www.bebitalia.it

Super-stylish contemporary Italian furniture by designers such as Antonio Citterio and Gaetano Pesce. Visit their website for details of their stores and stockists nationwide.

Boomerang For Modern

2040 India Street
San Diego, CA 92101
619-239-2040

www.boomerangformodern.com

Exceptional twentieth-century modern design. Deals in both well-cared-for vintage pieces and reissued classics.

Cassina USA

155 East 56th Street
New York, NY 10022
212-245-2121

www.cassinausa.com

This Italian manufacturer produces reissues of many iconic pieces of modern design, such as Gerrit Rietveld's Red/Blue chair and many Le Corbusier and Frank Lloyd Wright designs. Visit their website for details of their New York showroom and stockists nationwide.

Century Modern

2928 Main Street
Dallas, TX 75226
214-651-9200

www.centurymodern.com

Shop online or visit their large Dallas showroom for vintage chairs, storage, and lights, from rare pieces to unknown mid-century designs.

Chartreuse International

2609 First Avenue
Seattle, WA 98122
206-328-4844

www.modchartreuse.com

Selection of original twentieth-century classics and reissues by the likes of Charles and Ray Eames, Isamu Noguchi, Arne Jacobsen, and others.

Cherry

185 Orchard Street
New York, NY 10012
212-358-7131
A selection of vintage furnishings, fashion and accessories.

Circa 50

www.circa50.com

This extensive website offers reissues by modern retro designers such as Charles and Ray Eames, Verner Panton, Arne Jacobsen, Isamu Noguchi, and Ernest Race, as well as tableware by American ceramicists Russel Wright and Eva Zeisel. Furniture, clocks, lighting, and storage.

Design within Reach

455 Jackson Street
San Francisco, CA 94111
800-944-2233

www.dwr.com

Order modern classics from their online showroom, or visit their website for details of their 30-plus studios nationwide. Carries a good selection of modern classic children's furniture. The website sometimes offers sale goods or special offers.

Donzella

17 White Street
New York, NY 10013
212-965-8919

www.donzella.com

Modern twentieth-century furniture and decorative pieces by designers such as Paul Frankl, Edward Wormley, and T.H. Robsjohn-Gibbings.

Full House

428 Northampton Street
Easton, PA 18042
610-258-9330

www.fullhouse20.com

Original twentieth-century furniture, including pieces by Charles Eames, Ettore Sottsass, and George Nelson as well as their own exclusive designs.

Gansevoort Gallery

72 Gansevoort Street
New York, NY 10014
212-633-0555
Elegant mid-twentieth century furnishings, glass and ceramics. Many pieces are of museum quality.

Gomod

www.gomod.com

An online marketplace for buyers and sellers of mid-century modern design.

Good Eye

4918 Wisconsin Ave NW
Washington, DC 20016
202-244-8516

www.goodeyeonline.com

Vintage lighting, decorative objects, textiles, and housewares from designers including Robsjohn-Gibbings, Russel Wright, Arne Jacobsen, and Harry Bertoia.

Inform Interiors

97 Water Street
Vancouver, B. C.
Canada V6B 1A1
604-682-3868

www.informinteriors.com

Reissues of modern classics, as well as many contemporary pieces. Visit their website for details of their Seattle store.

Knoll International

76 Ninth Avenue, Floor 11
New York, NY 10011
212-343-4000

www.knoll.com

Classic twentieth-century pieces by Mies van der Rohe, Eero Saarinen, Harry Bertoia, and Florence Knoll. Visit their website for details of a retailer in your area.

Limn

290 Townsend Street
San Francisco
California, CA 94107
415-543-5466

www.limn.com

Contemporary furniture by Herman Miller, Ligne Roset, Cassina, and De Sede.

Lost City Arts

18 Cooper Square
New York, NY 10003
212-375-0500

www.lostcityarts.com

Original and reissued design classics from the 1930s to the 1960s.

Machine Age

354 Congress Street
Boston, MA 02210
617-482-0048

www.machine-age.com

Furniture from the 1940s to the 1970s.

Mecca Modern Interior

21a South Broadway
Denver, CO 80209
888-307-2600

www.meccainterior.com

European design classics.

Mode Moderne

159 North 3rd Street
Philadelphia, PA 19105
215-627-0299

www.modemoderne.com

Elegant mid-century modern furnishings.

Modernica

57 Greene Street
New York, NY 10012
212-219-1303

www.modernica.net

Modern classics from Herman Miller, Ligne Roset, and Artemide, as well as their own range of contemporary pieces. Visit their website for details of their other stores in Chicago and Los Angeles.

Modern Homes

2500 North Palm Canyon Drive
Suite B5B
Palm Springs, CA 92262
760-320-8422

www.shopmodernhomes.com

Everything you need to update, restore, or revive a mid-twentieth century or mid-century inspired contemporary home.

Modern House

7924 Lorain Avenue
Cleveland, OH 44102
216-651-3040
Vintage modern furnishings.

Modern Times

1538 North Milwaukee
Chicago, IL 60622
773-772-8871

www.moderntimeschicago.com

Home furnishings and accessories from the mid-twentieth century.

Modern Way

1426 North Palm Canyon Drive
Palm Springs, CA 92262
760-320-5455

www.psmodernway.com

Carefully-chosen furniture from the 1940s to the 1970s.

Quasi Modo

789 Queen Street West
Toronto, Ontario
Canada M6J IGI
416-703-8300

www.quasimodomodern.com

Modern furniture by renowned designers and manufacturers.

ReGeneration

38 Renwick Street
New York, NY 10013
212-741-2102

www.regenerationfurniture.com

Mid-century vintage furniture, with a focus on the 1950s. Specializes in pieces by American and Scandinavian designers.

RetroModern

www.retromodern.com

An internet superstore of twentieth-century design, offering both new and vintage pieces.

Senzatempo

1655 Meridian Avenue
Miami Beach, FL 33139
305-534-5588

www.senzatempo.com

Designer furniture from 1930–1960, including designs by Charles and Ray Eames, George Nelson, Alvar Aalto, and many more.

Shaboom's

5533 West Glendale Avenue
Glendale, AZ 85301
602-842-8687

www.shabooms.net

Twentieth-century classic furniture, decorative arts, lamps, and ceramics.

Swank

45 East 7th Street
New York, NY 10003
212-673-8597

www.swank-nyc.com

New and vintage twentieth-century classics.

Vladimir Kagan

www.vladimirkagan.com

Mid-century modern pieces by Vladimir Kagan. Visit this website for details of stockists in your area.

PICTURE CREDITS

Endpapers: The London loft of Andrew Weaving of Century, www.centuryd.com; **1** The London loft of Andrew Weaving of Century, *www.centuryd.com;* **2** The home of the architect Knud Holscher near Copenhagen; **3** The home of Sean and Tricia Brunson in Orlando, Florida; **4 above** The Paris apartment of art director, stage designer, and designer Jean-Pascal Levy-Trumet; **4 below** The home of Sean and Tricia Brunson in Orlando, Florida; **5 left** The home of Mark and Kristine Davis, Palm Springs, CA.; **6** The London home of Steven and Jane Collins, owner of *Sixty 6* boutique; **7** The Paris apartment of Nicolas Hug; **8–9** The home of David Jimenez in Palm Springs; **10** The home of Mark and Kristine Davis, Palm Springs, CA.; **11** The London home of Steven and Jane Collins, owner of *Sixty 6* boutique; **12–19** The home of Joy and Courtney Newman, owners of Modernway, vintage furniture store, Palm Springs; **20–29** The Paris apartment of Nicolas Hug; **30–37** The London loft of Andrew Weaving of Century, *www.centuryd.com;* **38–47** The home of Mark and Kristine Davis, Palm Springs, CA.; **48–55** The New York home of Jonathan Adler and Simon Doonan; **56–63** The summerhouse of the architect Knud Holscher, near Ordrup Naes, Denmark; **64–71** The Alexander home of Bruce Mink in Palm Springs; **72–79** a private residence; **80–87** The home of David Jimenez in Palm Springs; **88–95** The Paris apartment of art director, stage designer, and designer Jean-Pascal Levy-Trumet; **96–103** The house of Greta and David Iredale in Surrey; **104–111** The home of Andy Marcus and Ron Diliberto in Palm Springs, CA.; **112–119** The London home of Steven and Jane Collins, owner of *Sixty 6* boutique; **120–127** An original Florida home restored by Andrew Weaving of Century, *www.centuryd.com;* **128–137** The home of the architect Knud Holscher near Copenhagen; **138–145** The home of Ellen Weiman and Dubi Silverstein in New York, designed by architects Ogawa/Depardon; **146–153** The home of Sean and Tricia Brunson in Orlando, Florida; **156** An original Florida home restored by Andrew Weaving of Century, *www.centuryd.com.*

BUSINESS CREDITS

Jonathan Adler
Tel: (office) +212 645 2802
Email: web@jonathanadler.com
www.jonathanadler.com
Pages 48–55.

Jane Collins
Sixty 6
66 Marylebone High Street
London W1M 3AH
Tel: 020 7224 6066
Pages 6; 11; 112–119.

Architect: Gilles Depardon
Ogawa/Depardon Architects
69 Mercer Street, 2nd Floor
New York
New York, 10012
Tel: + 212 627 7390
F: + 212 431 3991
Email: info@oda-ny.com
www.oda-ny.com
Pages 138–145.

Huf Haus
Tel: 0870 2000035
www.hufhouse.com
Pages 96– 103.

Knud Holscher Arkitekt
Knud Holscher Design
Vermundsgade 40
2100 Copenhagen Ø
Denmark
Tel: + 45 39 29 10 01
Email: khid@knudholscher.dk
www.knudholscher.dk
Pages 2; 56–63; 128–137.

David Jimenez
www.djimenez.com
Pages 80–87

Jean-Pascal Levy-Trumet
JPLT
2 rue Jean-Baptiste Clément
93170 Bagnolet
France
Tel: + 33 1 43 60 01 10
F: + 33 1 43 60 05 50
M: + 33 6 11 90 19 98
Email: jplt@jplt.net
www.jplt.net
Pages 4 above; 88–95.

Andy L. Marcus
A.L.M. Interior Design
935 Westbourne Drive, # 201
West Hollywood
California, CA 90069
Tel: + 213 716 9797
Email:alminteriordesign@earthlink.net
Pages 104–111.

Philippe Menager & Nicolas Hug
'Immobilier de Collection'
31 rue de Tournon
75006 Paris
Tel: + 33 1 53 10 22 60
M: + 33 6 11 51 31
and
Architecte: Christophe Murail
Murail Architectures
MA – agence de Paris
Email: christophe.murail@m-a.fr
www.m-a.fr
and
Sculptures: Sébàstien Kito
Tel: + 33 6 11 51 31 32
Pages 7; 20–29.

Bruce Mink
The House of Mink Vacation Homes
Tel: +213 591 1110
Email: BruceMink@thehouseofmink.com
www.thehouseofmink.com
Pages 64–71.

Modern Homes Design Showroom
Tel: + 760 320 8422
Email: sales@psmodhome.com
www.shopmodernhomes.com
Pages 5 left; 38–47.

Joy and Courtney Newman
Modernway
745 North Palm Canyon Drive
Palm Springs
CA 92262
Tel: + 760 320 5455
Email: Greco@earthlink.net
www.psmodernway.com
Pages 12–19.

Andrew Weaving
Century Design
68 Marylebone High Street
London W1M 3AQ
Tel: 020 7487 5100
Email: modern@centuryd.com
www.centuryd.com
Pages 1; 30–39; 120–127 and endpapers.

INDEX

PAGE NUMBERS IN *ITALICS* REFER TO CAPTIONS.

ACKNOWLEDGMENTS

I would like to thank everyone who made this book happen, especially Alison Starling, who listened to me in the first place and immediately understood the need for a new book on the way we live with retro and vintage design now.

This book would not exist if it were not for all the house owners who let Andrew Wood and myself into their homes. Thanks to Courtney Newman, who introduced me to Catherine Meyler of location agency Meyler and Co, who then put me in touch with all the home owners in Palm Springs. Special thanks go to David Jimenez, who, due to our delays, stayed over in Palm Springs to enable us to photograph his home. Thanks also to Bruce Mink, who left us to it!

There are many more people I'd like to thank by name, but space does not allow. I'm sure everyone knows how grateful and inspired I am by all the enthusiasm and willingness to help make this book a great one.

Of course, thanks to Rosemary Smale for holding the fort at the shop and to Ian and Gretel for keeping me sane at home!